2 BUSINESS VENTURE

TEACHER'S GUIDE

Dorothy E. Zemach

Nina Leeke

OXFORD
UNIVERSITY PRESS

OXFORD
UNIVERSITY PRESS

Great Clarendon Street, Oxford OX2 6DP

Oxford University Press is a department of the University of Oxford.
It furthers the University's objective of excellence in research, scholarship,
and education by publishing worldwide in

Oxford New York

Auckland Cape Town Dar es Salaam Hong Kong Karachi
Kuala Lumpur Madrid Melbourne Mexico City Nairobi
New Delhi Shanghai Taipei Toronto

With offices in

Argentina Austria Brazil Chile Czech Republic France Greece
Guatemala Hungary Italy Japan Poland Portugal Singapore
South Korea Switzerland Thailand Turkey Ukraine Vietnam

OXFORD and OXFORD ENGLISH are registered trade marks of
Oxford University Press in the UK and in certain other countries

ISBN: 978 0 19 457809 7

Printed in China

ACKNOWLEDGEMENTS

Cover image: courtesy Alamy/Image Source Black.

The author would like to thank the following for their generous help: Roger Barnard,
Brett Berquist, Alan Headbloom, Hiromi Kawamura, and English language
students at Sumitomo Electric Industries and Central Michigan University.

Contents

Introduction

Business Venture is for people who need to use English in everyday business situations. Language is presented in a simple, straightforward way that helps students to understand spoken English and encourages them to speak. *Business Venture* is an American English course combined with examples of International English.

HOW THE *BUSINESS VENTURE* COURSE WORKS

There are four course components:
- Student Book with Audio CD
- Teacher's Guide
- Workbook

Student Book

The 12 units in the Student Book form the core of the *Business Venture* course.

Each unit by itself represents about three hours of classroom time, making a total of around 40 hours. This total will partly depend on the students and your approach. It includes the Review units, and the Information gap activities at the back of the book (see below). It does not include the TOEIC® section, or the photocopiable activities or extra activities suggested in the Teacher's Guide.

Teacher's Guide

The guide provides notes on each module plus ideas for extra activities. At the back of the book there is a bank of photocopiable activities and two progress tests.

Workbook

The course can be supplemented using the Workbook. There are one or more Workbook activities for each Student Book module. Each Workbook unit has around two hours of additional study time. The activities can be done in class or as self-study.

The total study time for the Student Book + Workbook is approximately 60 hours.

Audio CD

The Audio CD contains all the listening activities in the units, the TOEIC® section, and the listening tests in the Teacher's Guide.

HOW THE STUDENT BOOK WORKS

The Student Book is made up of:
- 12 units
- 3 Review units
- Information gap activities
- TOEIC practice
- Listening scripts
- Answer key

12 units

For details on the units see *How a unit works* below.

Review units

There is a review unit after every four units. The review gives the students an opportunity to refresh their memories and consolidate their understanding of both the functional language and the vocabulary. The practice usually takes the form of gap fill exercises which can also act as tests if necessary. The answers are in the back of the Student Book.

Information gap

These are speaking activities that give the students further communication practice. They are based on similar contexts to those in the unit and prompts that give the activity a framework within which the students can interact. They can be found at the back of the Student Book.

TOEIC® practice

This is an optional part of the book for students who need to do further language work related to the TOEIC test. It is also an opportunity for students to have further practice in the four skills.

It is divided into the four sections of the test: Listening, Reading, Speaking, and Writing. Each section is divided into the various parts of the TOEIC test for each skill. The parts give students Examples and Exercises that closely mirror what they will encounter in the TOEIC test.

In class you can go through the Example, making sure students understand the Directions. Then let students read the Test Tactic and Test Tips boxes, which give guidance in approaching each specific part of the test and how skills are tested. Finally set the Exercise under test conditions. Further Study boxes give suggestions on ways the students can extend the exercises.

Further Practice boxes refer to the *Tactics for TOEIC®* (OUP) titles by Grant Trew which have a full set of practice activities for all aspects of the test. For more information on the TOEIC test, visit the ETS website: www.ets.org/toeic.

The listening for the Listening and Speaking sections are at the end of the Audio CD. Play the Audio CD when you see the CD icon in the text.

The Audio CD also has a code which will give you access to free TOEIC practice tests online at www.oxfordenglishtesting.com, the Oxford English Testing site.

Listening scripts

The scripts are helpful when you want to look at examples of the target language, check the answer to a listening activity question, and for the students to read for consolidation and practice.

The scripts are numbered by module and by the track number on the narration.

Answer key

All the answers to the unit activities, review units, and TOEIC sections are in the back of the book. Answers to the TOEIC Speaking and Writing sections are not provided as these need to be evaluated individually.

HOW A UNIT WORKS

The menu

The menu at the beginning of each unit gives details of:
* the language introduced in the modules
* the situations the language is used in
* the skills that are practiced.

See page 4 for an example. The language is introduced in the form of typical functional expressions such as *I'd like to show you …*, *Can we meet to talk about …?*, and *What line of business are you in?*.

The menu also lists the top 12 or so most useful vocabulary items that are introduced in the unit. The functional expressions and vocabulary are practiced again in the Information gap activities, the Review units, and the Workbook exercises.

The modules

The unit is divided into modules, one module per page. There are six or seven modules per unit, and each module is a short lesson of around 30 minutes, depending on the class.

Each module is divided into activities which are signposted in the margin with headings that tell you which skill is being practiced.

The first activity of each unit, e.g. Module 1.1, asks students to describe a photo. This is supplemented with suggested questions in the Teacher's Guide. The activity is designed to get the students thinking and talking about the unit topic, functional language, and vocabulary. This provides excellent practice for the TOEIC test.

The first listening activity introduces the first language item and gives examples of how the language is used in a typical business context.

The number next to the icon, e.g. ◉23 tells you which track it is on the Audio CD. The first listening activity is followed by listening and speaking activities that give the students more examples of the language being used and opportunities to use the language in similar contexts.

Further listening activities either introduce language related to the first listening or give the students more extensive listening practice.

The speaking activities at the beginning of a unit are usually fairly controlled and become less controlled towards the end of the unit. The final activity in the language section is often a game that provides enjoyable and freer communication practice.

The Culture file module

The unit ends with a Culture file which presents a topic of cross-cultural interest for discussion. Students examine their own cultural practices and learn about those of other countries. The input often comes in the form of a short reading which gives the students an opportunity to work on their reading skills.

HOW THE TEACHER'S GUIDE WORKS

The Teacher's Guide is made up of:
- notes for each unit of the Student Book
- photocopiable material for each unit
- two progress tests

Notes

The main part of the guide is a simple set of notes to help you plan each stage of each activity in a module. The guide is organized in the same way as the Student Book, i.e. by module number and skills heading.

From Unit 2 onwards each unit starts with a review activity to help the students recall and review the topics and language from the previous unit. It is also a chance for students who were absent to catch up. There are also separate entries for optional extra activities.

Photocopiables

Each unit has a photocopiable activity which gives the students additional speaking practice. This is a further opportunity for the students to consolidate their ability to use the language in the unit and to improve their fluency. It is also a chance for you to check their spoken English and help correct any target language they are still struggling with.

Progress tests

The two progress tests cover units 1–6 and 7–12. They practice both the skills and the language from the six units. They are divided into Listening, Written, and Speaking. The Speaking test is made up of three parts: Interview, Role Play, and Presentation.

HOW THE WORKBOOK WORKS

The Workbook is organized in the same way as the Student Book and Teacher's Guide. Each module in the Student Book has a Workbook module which has at least one practice exercise. The exercises give further written practice of the target language, both the functional expressions and the vocabulary.

There are three basic options for using the Workbook:
- self-study
- additional class work
- a combination of the two

The option you choose will depend on how much time the students have to study on their own, the total amount of class time, and to what degree you need to monitor the students' progress.

SPEAKING ACTIVITIES

Pair work and role play

The main reason for pair work and role play is to give the whole class an opportunity to speak.

The main difference between pair work and role play is that students 'become' someone else in a role play. This has the advantage of taking away the restrictions of being themselves, i.e. they feel less self-conscious and can communicate in contexts they would not otherwise experience.

Give clear instructions so that the students understand what they have to do. It is also a good idea to explain why they are going to do the activity, e.g. to practice using the phrase *What are you doing …?* to talk about future arrangements.

You need to decide what prompts the students can use, if any. These could be notes on the board, or notes the students themselves have taken. Less confident students might want to write out the conversation first. The aim is to get the students to gradually be able to use the language reasonably fluently without any prompts.

These sorts of activities also give you the chance to monitor, i.e. to listen to the students and note how well they are doing and what sort of problems they are having. Make sure you give the students feedback and that the students feel the activity is worthwhile.

You can assign pairs. The advantages of doing this are that you can:
- put a weaker and stronger student together
- make sure the students work with different people
- avoid a junior employee working with a senior

Alternatively students are often happy just working with the person next to them or choosing a partner. If there are an uneven number of students, you can join in to make a pair, or the students can work in a group of three.

It's rewarding for the students to perform in front of the class after they've practiced together, but do make sure that you choose pairs that can do the activity and are confident.

Discussion

You can encourage discussion at any stage of a unit or a lesson. The Culture files at the end of a unit are design to stimulate the most discussion by introducing aspects of various cultures that the students can contrast with their own.

If your students are not familiar with free discussion activities, you may want to give them some time to prepare what they want to say.

You can lead the discussion if you want to make sure that everyone has a chance to speak and to encourage quieter students to speak out. For classes with students that are comfortable with interacting, it is a good idea to let them take turns, ask questions, interrupt, and so on without you prompting.

1 Meeting people

MODULE 1.1

SPEAKING

Ask students to look at the photo and describe the people. For example, *Where are they? Does the woman know the man on the left? What is the person in the middle doing? How do you know?* As a lead-in to the Listening activity, ask students where businesspeople meet for the first time, e.g. when they visit a company, when they go to a sales conference; what questions they ask each other, and how they might start the conversation.

LISTENING

1   Students listen to the three conversations. To check answers, play the recording again, pause after each conversation, and ask a student where it takes place. Ask students *How do you know?* to elicit key words from the conversation or other clues such as sound effects.

2   Allow students time to read the expressions before they listen. With lower-level classes, model the expressions first, and have students repeat them in chorus. Check for appropriate intonation. Then do the exercise. If some students find this exercise difficult, play the recording again, and have quicker students raise their hands when they hear the expressions.

3   Ask students which expressions they use at the start or end of a conversation.

MODULE 1.2

LISTENING

Students listen to the conversations first with books closed or the text covered. Ask some simple questions about each conversation, e.g. 1 *What are their names? Where are they?* 2 *What are their names? What company does Yuji Tanaka work for?* 3 *Where are they going?* etc.

Then have students listen again and complete the sentences.

SPEAKING

1   Students practice the conversations in pairs. With lower-level students you may want to drill the sentences first.

2   Students practice the conversations again. This time they use their own names and the information given.

For further practice after this exercise, have students invent their own substitutions. Higher-level classes can try to invent substitutions on the spot. Lower-level classes can write them down first. Have students present their conversations to the rest of the class.

You can also introduce some new expressions for students to use when they practice, e.g.

May I introduce myself?
I'm sorry, I didn't catch your name.
I see you're with Konica. (e.g. reading a name tag at a reception)
I attended your presentation yesterday. It was very interesting.
Mr. Tajima suggested I introduce myself to you.

To personalize this activity, have students practice real-life situations in which they might need to introduce themselves in English to a colleague or client.

EXTRA ACTIVITY

Conversation starters

Students work in pairs or groups of three and write short conversations that might occur in the places mentioned in 1.1 and 1.2. Have students practice the conversations a few times, and then present them to the class, who guess where the conversations take place.

You could also give students props to use, e.g. a watch to elicit *Excuse me, do you have the time?*; a newspaper to elicit *Excuse me, may I have a look at the sports section?*; an English book to elicit *Excuse me, are you studying English?*

MODULE 1.3

READING

1 Students match questions to topics. As an example point out *Who do you work for?* and *Jobs*. If necessary, give students another example. If you have time, you could then get students to brainstorm other questions on the same topics and write them up on the board.

2 Discuss the questions, making students aware of the Anglo-Saxon preference for not talking about money or religion, if necessary.

LISTENING

Elicit *Who are Tom Mason and Teresa Hu? Where are they?*

Students listen to the conversation and complete the sentences.

SPEAKING

1 In pairs, students practice the conversation from the Listening exercise. You may like to model and drill question intonation if your students are weak at this. Point out that if English speakers want to keep a conversation going they will usually add a follow-up sentence or ask another question in return when they have answered a question. Show students how Tom Mason and Teresa Hu do this. Ask students to keep this 'plus one' strategy in mind as they do the next exercise.

2 In pairs, students look at the information gap activity and follow instructions. You can then have them present their conversations to the class. See the Introduction, page 4, for tips on doing information gap activities.

MODULE 1.4

LISTENING

1 Ask students to name the products they can see in the pictures and in pairs / small groups to talk about any companies they know that produce these products. Have one student in each group take notes. When they have finished, ask each group to report back to the whole class.

Students listen to the conversations. With lower-level classes, pause after each section to give students time to process the information and match the photos. To check answers, play the recording again, and pause after each conversation. Ask students *What company is he / she talking about? How do you know?*

2 Students listen again and complete the notes. You may want to pre-check / teach some vocabulary: *set up, expand, company, celebrity.*

Have students compare their answers with their partner and then give feedback. If the class had difficulty, you can play the recording again, pausing when necessary.

READING

Students read the company descriptions. Explain that the first description is for a manufacturing industry, and the second description is for a service industry. Point out the language for talking about company activities: *we produce …*, *we provide …*, company size: *we have ten offices …*, and future plans: *we plan to ….*

WRITING

Students complete the sentences with information about their own company. Circulate and help if necessary. With higher-level students you can have them add further sentences about their company.

If all students work for the same company, you can ask them to write about other famous companies, or you could brainstorm everything students can say about their company as a class, writing it up on the board, or having students write things up on the board. Alternatively, students could write about their own department.

SPEAKING

Students tell their partners about the company they've written about. Again, you could ask students to give their company description to the class.

For further practice students work alone or with a partner and write short descriptions of well-known local companies without naming them. Then students read their descriptions aloud in small groups or to the whole class, and the other students try to guess which company they are talking about.

This can also be done as a pair or small group activity. One student describes a well-known company and the other students guess the name of the company, e.g.

A *This company makes sports shoes. It's an American company. Its motto is 'Just do it.'*

B *Is it Nike?*

A *Yes, that's right. / No, that's not right. Try again.*

MODULE 1.5

LISTENING

Brainstorm with students different reasons for finishing a conversation, e.g. *you have to leave; you want to speak to someone else; you have finished your discussion; the conversation comes to a natural close*, etc.

Students listen to the conversations. As you check answers, ask *How do you know?* to focus students' attention on the target expressions.

SPEAKING

Have students stand and practice the conversations. Make sure students practice each conversation at least twice, and take both parts.

For further practice, give students other situations, e.g. leaving English class, leaving the office at the end of the day, saying goodbye to a friend or colleague at a train station, or let them choose their own situations. Students work in pairs and practice similar conversations. They can write them down if they wish. When they are ready, each pair presents its conversation to the class. Have the rest of the class listen to see which person decides to finish the conversation. Write any new or useful vocabulary on the board.

MODULE 1.6

READING

Students match sentences and responses. With higher-level students you can elicit additional responses. With lower-level students you may like to drill some sentences for pronunciation.

WRITING

Students, either individually or in pairs, put sentences into the correct order to make a conversation. Check as a class and give help if necessary.

SPEAKING

Students practice the conversation in pairs, Student A uses the existing questions, Student B answers using their own information. Encourage Student B to use *How about you? And you?* Change roles and practice again. For further practice students can change partners.

While students are practicing, circulate and help, if necessary. Check for appropriate intonation and pronunciation. See the Introduction, page 6, for further notes on role play activities.

EXTRA ACTIVITY

At a conference

Use photocopiable page A, page 53. Make a copy for each student and cut the page into parts 1 and 2.

Explain that everyone will be going to a conference and should create new identities for themselves. Write the titles (name, job, etc.) on the board, and demonstrate completing them with fictional information. You can elicit fictional information from students.

Give out part 1 and have students fill it in by themselves. Circulate and help where necessary.

Explain that they are alone at the conference and want to meet as many people as possible. Elicit phrases for starting, developing, and finishing a conversation from the unit. Students can look back to the language in 1.2–1.6 if necessary.

Tell students that they want to find out some particular information about the other people at the conference and give out part 2. Check understanding of sentences 1–5, e.g. *if Jill has traveled from Bangkok to the conference and I have traveled from New York, who has traveled the farthest?* Tell students to write in the name of the person for each sentence.

Students mingle as a whole class. You may like to play some soft music in the background to create a good atmosphere. Depending on the size of the class, you could set a time limit for each conversation, e.g. four minutes, and then make a signal for students to change partners.

While students are mingling, circulate and listen for frequent errors. You may like to do a correction slot on these at the end of the lesson / beginning of the next lesson.

Call an end to the activity when students have had the chance to speak to about five people, or when conversation is flagging. Gather feedback on who students found for each category. Of course, there may be disagreement about which is the 'best' job, etc. You could have students explain the reasons for their opinions, or you could just accept all answers.

MODULE 1.7

READING

1 You might need to act out the gestures, especially those involving movement, to make them as clear as possible.

2 Students work in groups to match each gesture with its meaning. Circulate and help, if necessary. Check answers with the whole class by reading the meaning and having students demonstrate the gestures.

To help students memorize the gestures, have one student in each group perform a gesture, while the other students say its meaning; then have one student call out a meaning, while the others make the gesture.

SPEAKING

1 Have students explain if these gestures have the same or different meanings in their countries. Remind students that gestures that are common in one country may be unknown or even obscene in another country, and that gestures should always be used with care. For example, in Japan, the *OK!* gesture stands for money, while in Brazil and Germany it is considered vulgar or obscene; to indicate *come here* in many countries in the Far East one would hold the palm down, not up, and wave the fingers or whole hand.

2 In multilingual classes, students from the same country can work together, although it is not necessary. Allow students some time to think. If necessary, help students by asking them to think of what they do with their hands when they greet someone, say goodbye, agree or disagree, count, wish someone good luck, etc.

For further practice, ask students to work in pairs or small groups and write a short conversation in which some gestures are used, and perform it for the class.

2 Telephoning

REVIEW

Making conversation

Write the following stages of a conversation on the board:

1 *Start the conversation*
2 *Introduce yourself*
3 *Talk about (the conference, your trip, the weather, your job, etc.)*
4 *Finish the conversation*

Ask students to give phrases that can be used for each stage. If necessary, they can refer to Unit 1 for help. For lower-level classes, write some of the phrases on the board. Then have students stand up. Tell them they have three minutes to complete stages 1–3. At the end of three minutes, call *Time!* or use a timer with a bell or buzzer. Students should then finish the conversation, and move on to another partner. When students have formed a new pair, start timing again. This activity can also be used after class breaks, at the end of a class, or to re-energize a class.

MODULE 2.1

SPEAKING

Ask the students to look at the photo and describe what the man is doing, where he is, and where he might be going. Ask questions like *How often do you make telephone calls for your job? How many telephone calls do you receive each day? Do you ever make / have you ever made calls in English? What is easy / challenging for you about talking on the phone?*

LISTENING

1 Give students time to read the instructions before playing the conversations. Read the names of the three people to model the pronunciation. Then play the recording. With lower-level classes, pause the recording after each conversation. Check answers by asking *What happens when Bob calls Mary O'Brien?*, etc.

2 Read the expressions aloud or give students time to read them silently. Then play the conversations.

If necessary, play the recording again and ask students to raise their hands when they hear each expression. Check answers by asking *When did you hear 'He's on another line'?*, etc. If students are unfamiliar with the expressions, have them read the three conversations in pairs, using the listening script at the back of the Student Book, for consolidation.

For further practice, say the first half of the expression and have students complete it without looking at their books, if possible. Students can also practice this way in pairs. Point out that these expressions are very commonly used in telephone conversations and that it would be very useful to memorize them.

MODULE 2.2

Note: When practicing the conversations in this unit, try to approximate the reality of the telephoning situation by having students sit back to back or have them hold their books in front of their faces so that they cannot see each other. If students have cell phones, they could call each other from different ends of the room or from different rooms; toy telephones and speaker phones could also be used.

LISTENING

Have students guess the missing words to complete the conversation. They then listen to the conversation and complete the sentences. In preparation for the next activity you may also want to elicit and highlight the receptionist's responses (writing these up on the board if necessary). Drill the conversation, modeling the polite intonation.

SPEAKING

Before students start the exercise, model the correct pronunciation of each name. Point out the correct pronunciation of Ms (/mɪz/), Miss (/mɪs/), and Mrs (/mɪsɪz/). Remind students to use Ms for all women, unless they already know which title the person prefers.

Students practice the conversations in pairs. After the initial practice, have them practice the conversations without looking at their books. As a lead-in to the next listening, have students look at the photo and ask them *Who is it?* and *Who is he talking to?*

LISTENING

With books closed, students listen to the conversation and answer the following questions: *Who is Bob speaking to? What is he calling about?* Then play the conversation again and have students complete the sentences. Again, in preparation for the speaking exercise you may want to elicit Mr Takahashi's responses and write them on the board. Drill the conversation modeling the polite intonation.

SPEAKING

Students practice the conversations in pairs. After the initial practice, have them practice the conversation without looking at their books. To personalize the activity, you can ask students to practice a similar conversation based on a real-life phone call they may have to make.

MODULE 2.3

LISTENING

Have students pay attention to intonation and tone of voice as they listen to the conversation.

SPEAKING

1   Have pairs practice the conversation several times. Student A could try to repeat B's message without looking at the book.

2   Elicit the difference between *ask* and *tell* – in this case *ask someone to do something* and *tell someone some information*. To concept check you could give students some messages, e.g. *Please call me back; my number is 333 4455*, and ask students whether you are asking or telling. Highlight the forms *ask someone to do something, tell someone something*.

3   While students practice the conversations, circulate and check that they are using *ask* and *tell* correctly.

With higher-level classes, have Student A cover Exercise 3 and repeat the message without looking at the book. If he / she does not understand the message, he / she should say *I'm sorry, could you repeat that?*

For further practice, have students invent their own messages. They can also use their own names and companies.

MODULE 2.4

READING

Ask *What is important when you take a phone message?* to elicit answers like *Getting the caller's name; Getting the caller's phone number; Getting the information correct*. Brainstorm with the class some advice for leaving a voicemail message, e.g. think about or write your message down before you make the call; remember to leave your name and phone number, both at the beginning and the end of the message; spell your name; give the important information first; don't give too much information, etc.

Ask students to read the messages.

LISTENING

1   Ask students to predict what kinds of mistakes they might find, e.g. times, days, dates, numbers. With lower-level classes, play the recording and have students listen and circle the part of the message that is wrong; then play the recording again and have them correct the mistakes. Play the messages as many times as necessary. Check answers by asking students to tell you the correct message.

2   Pause the recording between messages to give students time to write the answers. Students can compare their answers in pairs, and then check them by looking at the Listening script at the back of the Student Book.

EXTRA ACTIVITY

Finishing a call

1 Ask students *How do you know when to finish a telephone call?* to elicit answers like *When all the information has been exchanged; If one of the callers is interrupted*, etc. Remind students not to finish a call too abruptly in case the caller has another question, to exchange a few closing remarks, and to hang up gently. Brainstorm with the class some closing lines, e.g.

Well, thank you for talking with me.
Well, it's been nice talking with you.
OK, I think that answers all my questions.
OK, I'll see you this Thursday at 3:00.

In general, the caller should finish the call first but sometimes the recipient may need to finish the call, e.g. *I'm sorry, but I have to go to a meeting now*.

These phrases are often introduced by *Well, So*, or *Anyway*, followed by a pause.

2 To practice finishing a call, write the following situations on the board:
   A *Do you have any more questions?*
   B *Not at the moment.*
   A *(finishes the call)*

   A *We should get together for lunch sometime.*
   B *That sounds nice. (finishes the call)*

   A *Thanks for all your help.*
   B *You're welcome. (finishes the call)*

   Students work in pairs and practice finishing the call using an appropriate expression, tone of voice, etc.

   They can also use these expressions to finish a call with the telephone role cards extra activity below.

MODULE 2.5

READING

Give the class time to read the instructions and think about what they would say for each instruction. Then go through the instructions, eliciting the target language, and writing it on the board if necessary.

SPEAKING

See the Introduction, page 6, for further notes on the pair work activities.

Students work in pairs to practice taking and leaving messages. Remind them that messages need not have identical wording as long as the meaning is the same and names and telephone numbers are correct. The students taking the message should write it down and after the conversation the pairs should check to see if they have the same information.

Circulate and monitor correct use of the target language and appropriate intonation and tone of voice.

To personalize the activity, students can practice a similar conversation based on a real-life message they may have to leave.

MODULE 2.6

SPEAKING

Demonstrate the game first by having a student circle an extension number and modeling the conversation with the student for the class, demonstrating all the possible substitutions so that students understand what to do.

Students play the game in pairs. Have students circle their choices of extension numbers in pencil, so that they can do the activity again.

Circulate and help, if necessary. Make sure students use complete sentences. When the activity is over, check which student found the people they were looking for with the fewest calls.

EXTRA ACTIVITY

Telephone role cards

1 Use photocopiable page B, page 54. Students work in pairs. Use role play cards 1A and 1B to demonstrate the activity. First read the A and B cards aloud. Then take the A role yourself and have a higher-level student take the B role. Then give out the other role play cards. (You can give 1A and 1B to a lower-level pair.)

2 Give students a few minutes to read their cards and think about the expressions they will use. Students should use their own names, where appropriate. Student A begins the call by saying *Hello, this is Mr / Ms _____ from _____ .* Students should practice both roles. After they have practiced the role play a few times, have pairs present their conversations to the class.

3 Then students exchange role play cards. Continue until each pair has had a chance to practice at least three of the role plays.

4 Circulate and help, if necessary. Make a note of any mistakes and write them on the board when the activity is over. Have students correct the mistakes, and then practice the correct forms in pairs.

MODULE 2.7

READING

Ask students to brainstorm in small groups or as a whole class different ways that business people communicate with each other at work, with co-workers, suppliers, customers, etc., e.g. the Internet, in person, phone, e-mail, etc. Write the answers on the board. You could make this into a competition to see which pair / group came up with the greatest number of methods. In multilingual classes you could ask students if certain types of communication are favored more than others in their countries.

To preview the reading you can also elicit the advantages of the different methods of communication mentioned.

Read through and check understanding of the four statements with students. Then students read the texts and try to match the texts with the statements. Have students compare their answers in pairs and then give feedback. After answering vocabulary questions, you can then ask students which of the four people they most agree with / are most similar to.

SPEAKING

a Students make a list of all the methods of communicating from the reading (and from the list on the board if there were more) and rank them according to how often they use them.

b In pairs they brainstorm situations in which one method is the best and then give feedback. Talk about the situation in the example and ask if they agree that a cell phone would be best. If students are stuck for ideas, give examples of situations and elicit the best form of communication for them, e.g. a negotiation between people in three different countries. This can lead on to a general discussion of the advantages and disadvantages of the different methods if you have time.

3 Schedules and appointments

REVIEW

Telephone messages

Write on the board:

A (Give company name.) This is _____ speaking. How may I help you?

B Yes, this is _____. Could I speak to Mr King?

A I'm sorry, he's not in right now. Can I take a message?

B Yes. Could you ask / tell him to _____?

A Certainly. I'll ask / tell him to _____ as soon as I see him.

B Thank you. Goodbye.

A Thank you for calling. Goodbye.

Students work in pairs. Give them a few minutes to think of a message to leave. Make sure students play both roles.

MODULE 3.1

SPEAKING

Ask students to look at the photo and describe what the man is doing. Ask *Do you use an electronic device to organize your schedules and appointments? How do you usually arrange appointments? What kind of information do you need to give / receive?* Explain the different names for this type of device to students, e.g. PDA (Personal Digital Assistant), Palm (a trademark), and handheld (generic).

LISTENING

1 Play the conversation once with books closed. Then have students listen again, and answer the question. Ask *What are Diane and Ken going to talk about at their meeting?*

2 Students look at the table and listen again in order to complete the information. Check answers by asking *Who is giving a presentation? What time?* etc.

SPEAKING

Point out that the present continuous tense is used to talk about future arrangements, especially when the time and place have been decided.

Model the question and answer, then have students practice asking and answering similar questions in pairs. Monitor for form and pronunciation, pointing out and encouraging the use of the contractions (*he's, she's*).

MODULE 3.2

WRITING

Students work in pairs. When they have finished, write on the board: *What date is tomorrow / the day after tomorrow?* etc. Use these questions to check answers. Practice days and dates by having students give full answers, i.e. *Tuesday March 7th, Wednesday March 8th,* etc. They can use either *March 7th* or *March the 7th.*

If necessary, practice pronunciation of ordinal numbers (especially *twelfth* and *twentieth*) by modeling the pronunciation yourself and then asking students to repeat in chorus and individually.

For further practice, set another day on the calendar as "today", and have students do the exercise again.

To personalize the activity, use copies of a calendar or students' own diaries. Have students use the real date or choose a day to be "today", and practice again using the questions on the board. They can also ask about future holidays or events in their own lives, e.g. *What's happening the day after tomorrow? When is our next class? What are you doing next weekend?* etc.

SPEAKING

In order to make sure that students understand what to do, demonstrate the start of this activity with one student for the class first. Remind students to answer in complete sentences and to use the present continuous tense. Circulate and check that students are using prepositions correctly, e.g. *next weekend* not *on next weekend*.

Note: It is possible to say both *on Monday* and *Monday*; *on the weekend* is American English, while *at the weekend* is British English.

Students can extend the exercise by asking and answering *yes / no* questions, e.g. *Is Diane attending a sales meeting next Monday? No, she's attending a sales meeting today* or *No, she's visiting customers next Monday.*

MODULE 3.3

LISTENING

Play the conversation first with books closed and have students listen for when they agree to meet. Play the recording again, using it as a model for students to repeat and practice pronunciation. Pay attention to intonation used for questions.

SPEAKING

1 Students practice the conversation in pairs. Make sure they practice both roles and have them repeat it several times. Encourage students to speak as much as possible without looking at the book.

2 Students practice the conversation again, using their own names, and the information from the table. To make the situation more realistic you can have students sit back to back or even use their cell phones to call each other. Circulate and monitor for difficulties of form or pronunciation.

To personalize the activity, you can again have students use their own diaries and give real reasons for meeting and for not being able to meet.

MODULE 3.4

LISTENING

1 Ask students what type of information is missing in blanks 1–5 to elicit *activities*. Play the recording giving the students enough time to fill in the missing information.

2 Ask students what type of information is missing in blanks 6–10 to elicit *dates* and *times*. Play the recording several times, if necessary, to give students time to write the answers. Have students check their answers in pairs or threes. As a final check, have students follow the listening script at the back of the Student Book as they listen.

For question and answer practice students can ask and answer questions about the schedule, e.g. *When does the recording session start? What are they doing next Monday at 6:30 p.m.?* etc.

EXTRA ACTIVITY

What's showing at the Plaza?

Bring to class English-language movie theater, concert hall, or play guides for the town or city you are in, English-speaking cities, and / or cities that students might visit on business trips. You can often download this kind of information from the Internet.

Students work in pairs. Give each pair a copy of the same guide, or have them share one copy. Students ask and answer questions like *What's showing at the Plaza tonight? Are there any concerts this weekend? Are there any matinee showings of _____? Can you use a movie pass for _____? How much do box seats cost?* etc. Encourage students to practice the time expressions introduced in this unit.

If you are in an English-speaking country, give your students the telephone numbers of theaters, museums, concert halls, etc. that have recorded information. For homework, ask students to find out specific information, e.g. which shows are scheduled for certain days, performance times, ticket prices, etc. Alternatively, give them the web address of a theater / what's on guide etc and have them find out specific information from the website.

MODULE 3.5

SPEAKING

1 Lead-in by asking students if they ever have to reschedule a meeting and what they might say. Give them time to look at the instructions and think about what they would say for each instruction before eliciting their responses. Most of the exponents needed have been practiced earlier in the unit, except for *Explain the situation…* and *Say you understand*, so pay attention to these and write up models on the board. You may like to point out the custom of apologizing for changing the schedule and model the appropriate polite intonation for doing so. Students then practice the conversation in pairs.

2 Make sure they take both roles. Circulate to check for difficulties and pay particular attention to polite intonation. Round off the activity by asking pairs when they are going to meet.

MODULE 3.6

SPEAKING

Read the instructions aloud while students read them silently to make sure everyone understands the task. You may want to demonstrate the start of the exercise with one student for the class, emphasizing that they shouldn't look at each other's information. As students do the exercise circulate and help, if necessary. Make sure each student writes down each appointment. If students have difficulties, write the following repair sentences on the board:

A *Let's go back a bit. What's he doing on the 22nd? / When is he having a check-up?*

B *Wait a minute, could I check something? Is the trade fair on Friday the 15th?*

Have students check answers by comparing books. For further practice you could check answers by giving true / false statements about Lee's schedule, e.g. *He's sailing on Friday July 15th*, and having students correct you if your statement is false.

Alternatively with lower-level classes or in a subsequent lesson, have students work with a new partner and take the other role.

MODULE 3.7

READING

Ask students to read the information about each country. Answer any vocabulary questions. If possible, have a world map available and point out the location of each country.

SPEAKING

Give students a few minutes to re-read the information before they begin. Circulate and check that students are using the auxiliary verbs for forming questions: *is / are / do*.

WRITING

If pairs have trouble thinking of ideas, have them join another pair. Circulate and help with ideas, if necessary, e.g. *What is the most common time for lunch? Is Monday morning a good time to meet? Is Friday afternoon a good time to meet? How late in the afternoon do people hold meetings? Do people ever meet outside the workplace? Where? How long does a typical meeting last? When do most people go on vacation? For how long?* etc. Finally, have students share their ideas with the whole class and write a list of useful information on the board.

EXTRA ACTIVITY

Can you join me for lunch?

1 Use photocopiable page C, page 55. Give each student a copy of the page. Read the instructions and the conversation with the class and give them a few minutes to write their own ideas for appointments, if they wish. Then model the conversation with a higher-level student. Explain any new expressions, e.g. *I'll pencil you in* = I'll write my appointment with you in my diary but it could change; *Something's come up* = I need to change our appointment because I have another appointment.

2   Remind students that they should make eight
    appointments with other students. (You can
    decrease or increase the number of appointments
    according to the time available.) Have the whole
    class circulate and make appointments. After
    they have made an appointment with one person,
    students should change partners. If you have fewer
    than nine students in your class, they can make
    two or more appointments with the same person.

3   Continue until the first person has made eight
    appointments or at least half of the class has
    finished. Then have students sit down and talk
    about their schedules in pairs, e.g.
    A *What are you doing on Monday?*
    B *I'm having lunch with _____ at 1:00, and*
    _____ is showing me how to use the new
    software at 3:00.

Variation: After students have made two or three
appointments, stop the activity. Tell them that
you are their boss and would like to make an
appointment with each student. They must cancel
any existing appointments in order to see you.
(Be sure to choose a time when they already have
an appointment by quickly looking at what they
have written down.) Students must then find the
person with whom they had the first appointment
and change the time, using the sentences at the
bottom of the photocopiable page for changing an
appointment.

Then circulate and ask different students to come
to see you in your office.

4 Company performance

REVIEW

Talking about appointments

Write on the board:

A *What are you doing tomorrow / the day after tomorrow / this Friday / next Thursday, etc.?*

B *I'm _____ing.*

Students ask and answer questions in pairs. They do not need to give real information; the important thing is to practice using the time expressions and the present continuous. Give students a few minutes to practice and then have them report their partners' plans to the whole class. Write this sentence on the board for students to use: *I spoke to Mr. / Ms. _____ . He / She is _____ tomorrow / this Friday*, etc.

MODULE 4.1

SPEAKING

Look at the photo. Ask *What is she doing?* to elicit *Giving a presentation / Explaining something.* Accept any reasonable answers. Ask *Do you ever give presentations? What about? To whom? Do you use graphs, charts, or other visual aids?*

LISTENING

1 Try to elicit the present tense and past participle forms of *rose* and *fell* and write them up for students' reference. As a final comprehension check when students have finished the exercise, have them work in pairs to quiz each other on the new phrases by asking *What does "rise slightly" mean?* to elicit the answer *It means to go up a little.* Students should try to answer without looking at the book.

2 Explain the meaning of the department vocabulary if necessary. Play the recording several times if necessary. With lower-level classes, pause the recording after each graph is described. Check answers by asking students to make sentences about the graphs, e.g. *Home improvement sales rose slightly*, etc.

3 For further practice with higher-level classes, brainstorm additional verbs and adverbs to describe upward and downward movement in graphs, e.g. upward: *increase, grow, soar;* downward: *decrease, decline, drop;* adverbs: *dramatically, somewhat, gradually.* Write new vocabulary on the board. Encourage students to use these words as well as the ones presented in Exercise 1 in the rest of the unit. You could also demonstrate the use of *from…to, to,* and *at* for describing graphs, e.g. *Sales rose from 1m to 2m, Sales remained constant at 2m*, using the graphs in 4.1 as reference.

MODULE 4.2

SPEAKING

1 Give students time to study the graph before they begin. They can refer to the vocabulary in 4.1 first if necessary, but should then repeat the exercise without referring back.

2 Tell students that it is helpful to listeners if they pause slightly after saying large numbers, especially when saying two or more large numbers close together. This gives listeners time to process the information. Draw students' attention to the use of the different prepositions: *from, to, at.*

Have students repeat the exercise by talking about all five months in a row to prepare them for the next activity.

3 Circulate and help, if necessary. Make sure that students don't look at each other's books. They can check answers afterwards by comparing books or describing their partners' graphs back to them.

EXTRA ACTIVITY

Describing graphs

1   Use photocopiable page D, page 56. Give each student a copy of the photocopiable page.

2   Students work in pairs. Together they invent a name for the company and the product it makes.

3   Student A completes the graph labeled "Total sales" and Student B completes the graph labeled "Total expenditure". They should not show each other their completed graphs. Students can use the graphs in sections 4.1 and 4.2 as examples for completing these graphs.

4   Student A describes his / her graph to Student B, who completes the total sales graph on his / her sheet. Then B describes his / her graph to Student A, who completes the total expenditure graph on his / her sheet.

5   To check that they have completed the graphs correctly, students compare their sheets. After checking the graphs, they calculate together whether the company made a profit or loss for the years 2003–2008.

6   Repeat steps 2–5 with the graphs labeled "Units made" and "Units sold". When they have checked the graphs, they calculate together whether the company produced a surplus or sold off existing stock.

MODULE 4.3

LISTENING

See the Extra activity below if students need more practice in dealing with large numbers.

Write the figures on the board in order to check answers. Ask students to read out the figures in order to highlight the ways of saying percentages, prices, and fractions. You may want to write up some more examples here.

For further practice you could play a dictation game: divide the class into teams, assign each team part of the board, dictate a list of numbers (relatively quickly, depending on the speed of the class), team members take it in turn to write up their number, and the team to finish first and / or most accurately wins.

SPEAKING

While students do the quiz in pairs, monitor and check that they are saying the figures correctly.

EXTRA ACTIVITY

Practicing large numbers

This activity will help students who may have trouble understanding and saying large numbers.

1   If necessary, remind students of the basic method of counting in English. Write on the board:

$$10 = ten$$
$$100 = one\ hundred$$
$$1,000 = one\ thousand$$
$$10,000 = ten\ thousand$$
$$100,000 = one\ hundred\ thousand$$
$$1,000,000 = one\ million$$
$$1,000,000,000 = one\ billion$$

Give students a variety of similar numbers to practice, e.g. 50; 70; 400; 8,000; 61,000; 200,000; and so on.

2   Explain that in English, numbers are read in groups of three or fewer. Remind students to pause slightly after the comma, and that they can say *and* after the hundreds figure. Write on the board:

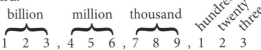

Model this number for students, writing *and* in the correct place as you speak. Practice the number for a few minutes until they begin to say it fairly easily and fluently.

3   Then write some large numbers on the board for students to practice. If they have problems, point to the appropriate place in the chart so that they can self-correct.

4   Put students in pairs. They should write five large numbers in their notebooks, and take turns dictating their numbers to their partners, who write them down. They check answers by comparing notebooks. If they need further practice, have them change partners and repeat the exercise.

MODULE 4.4

LISTENING

Lead in with books closed by asking *What's important when choosing which car to buy?* In this way you can elicit and / or explain potential new vocabulary, e.g. *emissions.* Then have students look at the table and ask them questions such as *Which is the most expensive car? Which is more powerful, the Hyundai or the Mazda?* in order to check comprehension of these comparative and superlative adjective forms.

With books closed, students listen to the conversation and answer the question *Which factors do the two people discuss?* Then play the recording again and have students follow in their books. If you want to work on pronunciation, you can then drill the conversation using the recording as a model, pausing after each sentence for students to repeat.

In preparation for the next activity, make a comparatives and superlatives table on the board, eliciting the forms of the adjectives given in the book. Highlight the forms *cleaner **than*** (as learners often confuse this with *as* or *like*) and ***the*** *cleanest* (as learners may omit the article). Ask students when we use *-er / -est, -ier / -iest,* and *more / most* (one syllable words, two syllable words ending in *y,* other two syllable words and words with more than two syllables). You may also want to remind students of the irregular forms of *good* and *bad.*

SPEAKING

In pairs students continue the conversation, comparing the cars using the adjectives given. Monitor and pay close attention to the correct comparative and superlative forms. With lower-level groups you can give more support by making sentences as a class first and writing up some of these as examples on the board.

For further practice, you could ask students to talk about what's important when buying something else, e.g. an apartment, a computer, a cell phone, and have them compare different products.

MODULE 4.5

READING

Give students time to study the graphs and try to match the sentences by themselves first. They can then check their answers with their partner. You can further practice the difference between *by* and *to* by drawing simple graph axes on the board and making some statements, e.g. *Sales rose by four million in June,* and having students mark the correct figure on the board (or tell it to you).

LISTENING

1 Play the recording with books closed. Ask *What is the presentation about? What three companies does he talk about? What years does he talk about?* Then open books and do the exercise. If necessary, pause the recording to allow students to write down the answers. Check answers as a class and write them on the board.

2 Play the recording and do the exercise. Students can check answers in pairs. Play the presentation again and have students listen and read the Listening script in the back of the Student Book. They should pay attention to intonation and pauses in these expressions and in the speech as a whole in preparation for the next section.

SPEAKING

Give students plenty of time to prepare. This stage could also be done for homework. Students present the figures for either Hyundai or Isuzu to their partner. Circulate and check for use of the expressions and appropriate stress and intonation.

You could then have students present to the class. For a presentation atmosphere, draw the chart on the board, so that students can refer to it and point to the appropriate information as they speak. Remind students to use appropriate pauses and to make eye contact with their audience.

MODULE 4.6

READING

Start by introducing the topic "100 Best Companies to Work For" and asking students what makes a company a good place to work. This leads in to elicitation / pre-checking of potential unknown vocabulary, e.g. *benefits*, *flexible*, *pension*. Then have students read the text and find out why Wegmans is such a good place to work.

To encourage cooperation and dealing with unknown vocabulary, you could put students in groups of four and have each student read a paragraph aloud. Ask students to underline any unknown words as they read. They should help each other or try to guess the meaning of the unknown words before consulting a dictionary. Explain any words which are still causing problems.

Check answers as a class.

SPEAKING

Students can discuss all or some of the questions in their groups. At the end of the discussion have students share their answers with the whole class.

For further practice or for homework, have students write a short paragraph about working conditions in their company.

5 Products and services

REVIEW

Large numbers

Students work in groups of 5–7 and sit in a circle or a line. Choose one student to begin. This student writes a six-digit number on a piece of paper but does not show it to anyone. He / She then whispers the number to the student on his / her left only once. That student writes down the number, and whispers it to the person on his / her left, and so on. The last person reads the number aloud. The number should, of course, be the same as the number written by the first student. Choose a different student to begin, and repeat the activity.

MODULE 5.1

SPEAKING

Look at the photo. Ask *Where are they? What are they doing? What do you think they're talking about?*

Ask students what features they might ask about if they want to buy a cell phone.

LISTENING

1   Check students are familiar with each of the features listed before playing the conversation. You can check answers by playing the recording again and having students call out / raise their hands when they hear the feature mentioned.

2   To make the exercise more active, you may like to have students guess the missing question words before listening, and then listen to check their answers. With higher-level classes you can play the recording again with books closed and have students listen for questions.

Then have students practice the questions and answers in pairs several times. Circulate and monitor for difficulties.

MODULE 5.2

WRITING

Students work in pairs to write questions for the answers. Some of the questions in 5.1 will help them. You may need to assist for other questions. You may like to drill the questions and answers for pronunciation and intonation in preparation for the next activity. Have students practice reading the conversation in pairs, looking at their books as little as possible.

SPEAKING

Students practice similar conversations in pairs using the products given. Monitor and check for correct pronunciation and intonation. To extend the activity you could have students practice the conversation with a product of their own choosing.

EXTRA ACTIVITY

Commercials

1   If you have access to English-language TV, record a few TV commercials or access some commercials on the Internet. Have students watch and listen for information such as product price, special offers, and ordering information. Write common or useful phrases on the board.

2   Put students in groups of 3–4 to script their own commercial for a product of their choice. Circulate and help with vocabulary and ideas, and to make sure that everyone is fully involved. When they are ready, have groups perform their commercials for the class, or record them with a video camera and show them to the class in a subsequent lesson.

Alternatively, you could record some commercials in the local language and play them with the volume down. Students must write down in English what is happening, and what they think is being said.

MODULE 5.3

READING

If students work for the same company, elicit the company information (business type, company HQ, employees, activities) and write it on the board in preparation for the activity. Alternatively, you could use a very well-known company or your language school (if you work for one) as an example. Then have students complete the information on their two companies.

SPEAKING

1   Try to elicit the questions before having students look at them in their books. Circulate and monitor, especially for correct question intonation.

2   Make sure that students don't look at each other's information, but instead ask appropriate checking questions, e.g. *Sorry, can you repeat that? Is that 50,000 or 15,000?* in order to take down correct notes.

3   If students are stuck for ideas, they can present their own company or you can give them some ideas.

EXTRA ACTIVITY

Internet companies

If your students have access to the Internet, ask them for homework to visit the website of a company which sells products (e.g. books, antiques, clothing) or provides services (e.g. financial advice, travel services) on the Internet, and write a brief report about it to share with the class. Ask students to report on what the company sells / provides, how many and what kind of products / services it provides, any special features of the website and / or company, how one can order and pay, whether the company can ship overseas, what languages the website is in, etc. If appropriate, students should also visit the English-language website of their own companies. Students then present their information in small groups or to the whole class.

MODULE 5.4

LISTENING

1   Ask students what kinds of things people might talk about if they meet at a conference. With books closed, play the conversation and have students listen for which topics are mentioned. Play the recording again and have students complete the exercise. If there are difficulties or disagreements about the correct answers, you can play the recording again and have students stop you when they hear the answer.

2   Students complete the questions individually or in pairs. To ensure that everyone has a note of the complete question forms you can write them on the board (or have students write them on the board).

SPEAKING

Students practice the questions and answers. Circulate and monitor for the correct question forms and intonation. Encourage students to refer to their books as little as possible.

MODULE 5.5

LISTENING

Ask students to think about visiting a client to talk about a product or service. Ask *What kinds of things make a good impression on the client?* e.g. using polite language, thanking the client for his / her time, giving enough but not too much information, etc. and *What kind of information should you give?* e.g. a description of the product or service, any special features, any promotional special offers, contact information, etc. Ask them to imagine being a client who would like to organize language training for their employees, and ask *What kinds of questions would you ask?* e.g. about prices, schedules, location, etc.

Students complete the exercise. For further practice you can have them listen again and try to note the answers to the questions. Students can then practice the conversation in preparation for the next activity.

SPEAKING

Pairs practice similar conversations based on the information-gap material. Monitor and pay particular attention to the question forms and polite intonation. For further practice, students can swap roles.

To personalize the activity, you could ask students what kind of questions a client would ask a representative of their company, if appropriate.

MODULE 5.6

SPEAKING

Student B should turn immediately to page 92 so that he / she does not accidentally see A's list of products.

Read the instructions with the class and make sure that they understand what to do before they begin. Then ask two students to model the example conversation while the other students follow it in the book.

Call *Time!* after five minutes and check which pair has guessed the most products. You could also allow students to play the game until they are able to guess all or most of the products.

If students have questions about the vocabulary or products on their lists, have them raise their hands and ask you quietly so that their partners don't hear what they are asking about or they can consult their dictionaries.

You can extend the activity by having students come up with their own ideas for products to describe.

MODULE 5.7

Look at the photos. Ask students *Where do you think the two people are? How do you think they feel?*

READING

Have students work alone to do the questionnaire. Encourage them to think about or write down some notes about why they agree or disagree.

SPEAKING

1 If students want to give answers like *It depends*, encourage them to be precise about what their answers depend on.

2 Have each group discuss the same questions or give each group a different question to discuss. Make sure one person in each group takes notes

on the group's ideas to report back to the class. Remind students that they do not need to agree; the note-taker should simply write down conflicting viewpoints.

Possible answers:

a To provide technical expertise to the overseas company; to get training from the overseas company; to improve an employee's ability to interact in a foreign language / different culture, etc.

b A person who is flexible, adaptable, willing to learn, and able to handle stress well, etc.

c Assistance with relocation, finding suitable housing and schools, setting up house, language instruction for spouse and children, help with paperwork, etc.

d Language, culture, cost / convenience of living, homesickness, children falling behind in schooling, re-entry shock when they return home, etc.

To personalize this discussion ask if any class members have worked abroad or with foreigners, and if they have any experiences they could share. Ask if any students expect to work abroad in the future, either in the short term or the long term, what challenges they anticipate, and how they might prepare for those challenges. If you have worked overseas, consider sharing your experiences. Try to ensure both positive and negative experiences are discussed.

EXTRA ACTIVITY

Promoting a product

1 Use photocopiable page E, page 57. Students work in small groups. Give each group one of the products on the photocopiable page. Make enough copies so that each student has his / her own.

2 Students discuss ways of promoting their product. Some ideas are given on the photocopiable page. Students should complete the sheet with ideas of their own, e.g. any special features or any other information about the product, and also give a price for the product.

3 Make new groups so that each group contains one student from each of the original groups. Each student in turn then describes and promotes his / her product to the group. Other students can ask for further information about the product, if they wish.

6 Talking about decisions

REVIEW

Describing products and services

Write the names of some everyday products on slips of paper, e.g. lightbulb, printer, knife, whiteboard, flashlight, dictionary, notebook, camera, etc. Give each student a slip of paper. They must not show it to anyone. You can also provide blank slips of paper for students to write the names of products of their own choice.

Write on the board:

A *I'm thinking of a product for the home / office / school, etc.*

B *What's it made of? / How big is it? / How much does it cost? etc.*

Students work in pairs or small groups, taking turns to ask and answer questions and guess the products.

MODULE 6.1

SPEAKING

Ask students to describe the situation. *Where might they be? What kind of meeting is it?*

LISTENING

1   Ask students whether they know any American motorcycle brands, e.g. Harley-Davidson or Victory, then have them listen with books closed. Students then read through the exercise before they listen again. Check answers by asking *What happened first / second / third / fourth?*

2   Explain that students will be listening for words or phrases that link two ideas. Before they listen, have students try to guess what words might complete the sentences. Then do the exercise. Check answers by asking students to read the completed sentences aloud.

MODULE 6.2

READING

Read the instructions and the example sentences aloud. Point out that the example sentences are simply four different ways of connecting the same

two statements of cause and effect. Have students underline the connectors *so / and / as a result / because*.

SPEAKING

1   Give students a few minutes to read the statements. While they do the exercise, circulate and check that they are using the connectors correctly. Have students repeat the exercise at least once, using different words each time to connect the sentences.

2   Encourage students not to ask about each statement in sequence so that their partners will have to listen carefully. Circulate and help, if necessary. Check that students form the past simple tense questions correctly, e.g. *Why did production increase?* and not *Why did production increased?* or *Why production increased?* and that they are using the irregular verbs *rise / rose* and *fall / fell* correctly. If they are having problems with these verbs refer them back to 4.1.

MODULE 6.3

LISTENING

Students look at the photo and the notes and listen with the conversation covered. Then give them time to read the conversation silently before they listen again, following the conversation in the book as they listen. If necessary, explain *objective*, *expand*, and *franchise*.

SPEAKING

1   Students practice the conversation in pairs.

2   Encourage Student A to memorize the three questions so that only Student B looks at the book.

3   Give students a few minutes to think of ideas and write them down. Circulate and help with ideas if students get stuck, e.g. buying a car / computer, choosing a college / apartment, changing jobs, etc. Lower-level students may need to take notes about their partners' decisions.

When students have finished, ask each student to talk about one other person's decision, e.g. *I talked to Mr / Ms _____ . He / she wanted to*

_____ *so he / she decided to* _____ . *As a result* _____ .

For variation, do the exercise as a whole-class activity by having students stand and circulate, talking to as many different people as possible in five minutes. You can give students an objective in this activity by having them find the person who made the biggest / best / worst decision. Or have students memorize the information about their own decision and present it to the class as a short speech.

MODULE 6.4

LISTENING

1 Look at the photos and ask students to describe what they see.

Play the recording. With lower-level classes, pause after each section. Check answers by having students ask and answer in pairs *What does company number 1 do?* etc.

2 Have students read the chart before they do the exercise. Answer any vocabulary questions. Ask students to try to match the objective, decision, and result with the correct company before they listen. Then play the recording, pausing between sections, if necessary. Check answers by asking *What was company number 1's objective? What was its decision? What was the result?* etc.

SPEAKING

Extend the activity by writing on the board:

(result) because (decision) in order to (objective)

e.g. *Brand recognition among young male shoppers increased because Gillette carried out a big advertising campaign in order to improve brand recognition.*

Have students read the information in this way to each other or to the whole class. For consolidation, students can write these sentences down.

MODULE 6.5

SPEAKING

1 Have students study the franchise operations. Deal with any vocabulary questions. Ask them to write down which one they would choose for their neighborhood / town and why.

2 Model the example conversation with a student. Draw students' attention to the Useful language. Then do the activity. Circulate and listen for mistakes. When the activity is over, write the incorrect sentences you heard on the board and have students correct them. Have the pairs report back on which franchise they agreed on and why. For further practice you could make this into a pyramid discussion: once students have reached a decision in pairs, they team up with another pair and try to reach agreement, then with another group / the class.

To extend the activity, ask students to make a list of things they would do to make their chosen franchise successful, e.g. SmoothJuice: *have a different "special juice" every day; offer a special lunchtime two for one offer; sell extra items like fresh fruit or cereal,* etc. Looking Glass: *sell designer clothes; offer budget lines; rent fancy dress costumes,* etc. Students can work alone or in pairs or small groups with other students who chose the same franchise.

As a variation, put students in small groups and tell each group to choose four or five of the franchises from Exercise 1 for a different location, e.g. a shopping mall in a city, the downtown area of a small town, an airport, a resort area. Give students ten minutes to choose the franchises and write down reasons why they chose certain franchises and not others. Then have a spokesperson for each group explain the group's choices to the class. Encourage students to give specific reasons, e.g. for a shopping mall: *We think a Looking Glass franchise would be successful because many parents like the convenience of shopping in malls, and it's easy for them to bring their children along.*

MODULE 6.6

READING

Have students brainstorm as a whole class answers to the two questions in the article *Who makes decisions at work? How do they make them?* Encourage students to think of as many possibilities as they can, but do not evaluate or give opinions on the suggestions at this point. Then ask four students to read the texts aloud or have students read them silently. Answer any vocabulary questions or allow students to consult a dictionary.

SPEAKING

1 If some students are reluctant or unable to pick one person to agree with, have them list the pros and cons of each person's position.

2 To discuss the questions, consider grouping students either by different nationality or job (in which case different opinions might arise immediately) or by the same or similar nationality or job (in which case different opinions may emerge later in the subsequent whole-class discussion); also take into consideration age and personality. Students who are hesitant about offering different opinions or who form opinions more slowly might prefer the latter grouping.

   a Have students give reasons for their answer.

   b Students who don't work can talk about companies they know, where their parents work, their school, a club or other organization to which they belong.

   c Have students give reasons for their choices. They can also include any decision-making styles that came up in the initial brainstorming.

For further practice, ask students which decision-making styles they would recommend for

   – a high school club
   – a family with children under twelve years of age
   – a family with children in their teens
   – a social or sports club for adults
   – your English class

Encourage students to suggest other situations for the class to consider.

EXTRA ACTIVITY

Chain of events

1 Use photocopiable page F, page 58. Students work in pairs or small groups. Make one copy for each pair / group and cut into individual cards.

2 Give one set of cards to each pair / group. Students shuffle the cards and then put them in a logical order. Note: in some places more than one sequence is possible.

3 Check answers with the whole class. Allow different sequences if they are logical.

4 Write the connectors on the board: *and / as a result / so*.

5 Then have each pair / group place the cards in a stack in the correct order, with the first card at the top. Student A should use a suitable connector from those on the board and try to recall the information on the second card without looking at it, e.g. *Jody had an idea for a new line of frozen vegetarian dishes, so she called her friend Jim.* If Student A cannot remember, the other students can help, but Student A must say the sentence. If no one can remember, they check the second card and Student A says the sentence. They then place the first card at the bottom of the pack and Student B repeats the procedure with the second and third cards. Continue like this to the end of the pack.

Note: Remind students that they should change nouns to pronouns, e.g. *Jody and Jim* to *they*; *the products* to *they/them*.

6 Now add *because* to the connectors on the board, and give an example of linking two items in reverse order, e.g. cards 2 and 1: *Jody called her friend Jim because she had an idea for a new line of frozen vegetarian dishes.* Then tell the class there are three more pairs of sentences which can be connected using *because*. The first pair / group to find and say them correctly wins.

Answers: (1) *Jody and Jim showed their products to several shops in the local shopping mall because they needed to find a store to carry their products.* (2) *The downtown store agreed to carry the products because they thought they were excellent.* (3) *Other stores wanted to sell the products because they were very popular.*

7 Complaints and problems

REVIEW

Business decisions

Write on the board:

Sports center: attract new members
Clothing company: get a more modern image
Video game company: sell more games to adults

This is a whole-class activity. Tell students *You are the manager of a sports center. You wanted to attract new members. What did you decide to do?* Give students a few minutes to think, and then ask each student in turn to answer *I decided to _____ .* Continue until every student has spoken or they have run out of ideas. Then move on to the next situation: *You are the manager of a clothing company …,* etc.

MODULE 7.1

SPEAKING

Ask *Where are they? What are they doing? How do they feel? Do you ever complain? What about?*

LISTENING

1 Read the instructions. Ask *Why might a customer complain to a wholesaler? What does a customer service representative do when he / she receives a complaint?* Have students read the sentences before they listen. Check understanding of *items* and *damaged*. Then do the exercise. Check answers by asking *What was the complaint in Conversation 1? What was the complaint in Conversation 2?*

2 Have students read the expressions before they listen. With lower-level classes model each expression and have students repeat them in chorus. Then do the exercise. Check answers by asking *What did you hear in Conversation 1? What did you hear in Conversation 2?*

MODULE 7.2

LISTENING

1 Have students work alone at this stage, as they will practice the conversation in pairs in Speaking 3.

2 Tell students to listen to A's (Sandy's) tone of voice. Remind them that it is important to sound polite and sincere when apologizing. Draw attention to the rising intonation on *The wrong amount?*

SPEAKING

1 To capture the feeling of being on the phone, have students sit back to back.

2 As students practice, circulate and monitor appropriate tone of voice and intonation.

3 If there is time, have students write more than one problem. After they have practiced in pairs, students could present their conversation to the whole class.

MODULE 7.3

LISTENING

As they listen, have students underline the polite words or phrases used by both speakers.

As the sentences in this conversation are quite long, you may prefer to do some choral repetition, especially with lower-level classes, i.e. read the conversation aloud in chunks, pausing between short sentences or after the comma in longer sentences, and have students repeat the phrases after you in chorus.

SPEAKING

1 Remind students of Sandy's polite tone of voice when she apologized, and to use the same tone when they practice the conversation. Circulate and monitor appropriate intonation.

2 Ask two students to read the conversation in Listening aloud while the rest of the class studies the order form. Ask students to point to the appropriate information on the form when they hear it mentioned.

Students can sit back to back to give the feeling of talking on the phone. Remind them to use a polite tone of voice.

3 In this activity students give two complaints during the same call. They could introduce the

second one by saying *I'm afraid there's also another problem*. Monitor and ensure that they don't look at each other's information.

MODULE 7.4

LISTENING

1 Look at each picture and ask *Where is this? What do you think he / she is complaining about?* With lower-level classes, pause the recording after each conversation. Play the conversations several times, if necessary.

2 With lower-level classes, play the recording and ask students to write the complaint, and then play it again for them to write the solution. Students can write notes instead of complete sentences. Pause the recording between conversations to give students time to write.

SPEAKING

Use this stage as a comprehension check. If students disagree about the answers, have them check the Listening script at the back of the Student Book.

For further practice, have students give each other a memory quiz after they complete this exercise. Write this exchange on the board for students to use:

A *Who had a problem with the _____?*
B *The woman / man in Conversation _____ .*

EXTRA ACTIVITY

Finding solutions

1 Have the whole class brainstorm common complaints that arise at work, school, or in other places, e.g. shop, theater, etc., or use the complaints in the Student Book in 7.4. Make a list on one half of the board.

2 Then have students brainstorm possible solutions. Ask higher-level classes to indicate which solutions are best for the customer and which are best for the provider; in some cases they may overlap.

On the other half of the board make a list of phrases which can be used to offer and request solutions. Tailor them to fit the complaints your students suggested above. Examples:

To offer solutions
I'll send out the order right away.
I'll send someone to fix that as soon as possible.
I'll replace it / them on Monday.
I'll send you a refund.
We can offer you a 10% discount on your next order.
We won't charge you for the _____ .
I assure you it won't happen again.

To request solutions
Could you send the order again?
Could you send someone to fix that?
Can you offer me a discount?
I'd like a replacement.
I'd like a refund.
I'd like to cancel the order.

3 Then have students work in pairs and practice complaints conversations, with Student A offering a solution at the appropriate point in the dialogue. Student B can accept the solution or request a different solution. After each conversation, students should change partners and practice again.

MODULE 7.5

SPEAKING

1 Ask students *What kinds of problems can you have in a hotel?* Write the ideas on the board to be used later in the role play, and add your own if necessary, e.g. no hangers in the closet, the room is smoky, no writing paper in the desk, etc. Check that students know *apologize* (verb) and *apology* (noun).

With lower-level classes, ask *What can you say to answer the phone?* to elicit the target language for the prompts before they do the role play. If necessary, write some of the sentences on the board. Lower-level students could also read the Listening script of Conversation 4 in 7.4 and use it as a model.

Remind students to use a polite tone when apologizing. Then do the role play.

2 After students have practiced several times, have them present one of their conversation to the class.

EXTRA ACTIVITY

Complaints conversation

1   Use photocopiable page G, page 59. Cut the page up and give one half of each conversation (the A card or the B card) to each student, taking care not to give the second half of a conversation to a student sitting close to the person with the first half. If you have an odd number of students, play a part yourself.

2   Tell students they each have one half of a telephone conversation. Student A is making a complaint, and Student B is dealing with the complaint. Have higher-level classes memorize their sentences and then collect the cards; lower-level classes can keep them for reference.

Note: The number in the bottom right corner of each card is for the teacher's reference only. Tell students to ignore it.

3   Have students stand up and circulate, trying to find the person with the other half of their conversation. Student A starts by saying his / her first line, then Student B says his / her first line. If the first lines seem to go together, A says the next line, and B gives the last line. Together they decide if their conversation makes sense. If it does, they should stand together and practice their conversation several times. If it doesn't, they should move on and speak to other students until they find the other half of their conversation.

When you see two students standing together, quickly check that they have the correct conversation. If they are mistaken, this will obviously cause problems for the rest of the class.

4   When all students feel they have found the correct partner, ask the pairs to recite their conversations while the rest of the students listen and say if they think the conversation is correct.

For further practice, students work in new pairs. Give them a new A or B card, and ask them to write appropriate original lines for the missing parts of their conversation. Then have them recite their conversations to the class.

MODULE 7.6

SPEAKING

1   Look at the pictures and ask *How do you think the people feel?* Write any feelings words students suggest on the board.

Check that students know the meanings of the ten feelings words – some of them may already have been listed on the board, but if students don't know them, let them consult a dictionary or give example situations that would elicit the feeling, but do not make a facial expression.

Then ask students to think about how English native speakers would look when expressing these feelings. Put students in pairs to discuss their answers. Then check answers with the whole class. Cultural differences may appear, e.g. an American smiles when happy, but a Thai or Japanese person also smiles when embarrassed. To encourage students to consider cultural differences ask *How does a person in your country look when angry / nervous, etc?*

2   Give students a few minutes to answer the questionnaire alone.

3   Students can work with a partner from the same country and compare answers, or if possible, with a partner from a different country.

4   Be ready with some information about your own or other countries in case students get stuck for ideas, i.e. in south-east Asian countries, business people tend not to show anger or other strong emotions openly, believing that displaying emotions shows lack of control, which is seen as a sign of weakness. Arabs are somewhat demonstrative, believing that strong emotions express one's sincerity and commitment. In Europe, the British, Scandinavians, and Germans are generally more reserved than Spanish, Italian, or French people.

5 If students don't work, you could ask them this in relation to their teachers, classmates, family, or friends.

For further practice have students write a simple questionnaire of five situations: How would you feel if you _____, e.g. got fired / won a big contract / got married / made a serious mistake at work / got lost in a strange city, etc? Then have students stand and circulate, asking their five questions of as many people as they can. The person answering should name the feeling: I'd feel _____, and if appropriate, make a facial gesture to accompany it.

To extend the activity, play "emotions charades" in small groups or as a whole class. One student acts out an emotion with facial expressions and gestures while other students try to guess what it is.

8 Checking progress

REVIEW

Making and dealing with complaints

Write the following situations on the board:

1 *A customer calls a computer store to complain that his / her new computer isn't working.*
2 *An office manager calls his / her supplier to complain about a photocopier.*
3 *A hotel guest calls the front desk to complain about a problem.*
4 *Your own idea.*

Students work in pairs to practice complaints conversations. With higher-level classes have Student A offer a specific solution to the problem.

MODULE 8.1

SPEAKING

Ask *Where are they? Who are they? What are they doing? Why are they visiting the construction site?* in order to try to elicit the idea of checking what has / hasn't been done.

LISTENING

1 Have students read the exercise before they listen. To check answers ask *Has Dan reserved the flight / made the hotel reservations yet?*, etc. to elicit *Yes, he has / No, he hasn't.*

2 Pause the recording to give students time to write. Then play the entire conversation again for students to check their answers. Ask two students to read the completed sentences aloud. Point out that Dan uses the contraction *I've* which is more common in speech, but that it is also possible to use the full form *I have.*

For further comprehension practice, ask *What did Dan do yesterday? What did Mr. Viana's assistant say to Dan? When is Dan going to arrange a car for Cindy?*

EXTRA ACTIVITY

Present perfect forms

This activity is useful for students who are not confident about the present perfect forms, and is a quick and simple way to practice using the present perfect with the indefinite time adverbs *already*, *yet*, and *ever* that mean 'at some / any time up to now', and to practice various past participle forms.

1 Write on the board:
   A *Have you already _____? / Have you _____ yet?*
   B *Yes, I've already _____. / No, I haven't _____ yet.*

2 Write some prompts on the board, e.g. *make the coffee / send the fax / write the report / see your boss / call your client / check your e-mail / have lunch / take a break / file the papers / photocopy the documents / order the parts / your own ideas.*

   Start by taking the A part yourself and call on students to complete the B part. Then ask two students to speak. Do this a few times until students know what to do. If students do not know the correct past participles, write them on the board.

3 Students practice again in pairs. Circulate and monitor.

4 Repeat the above procedure using the following exchange:
   A *Have you ever _____?*
   B *Yes, I've _____. / No, I've never _____.*

   Use prompts such as *visit Germany / see an English movie / be late to work / try Mexican food / take a boat trip / win a contest / change jobs / move to another city / your own ideas.*

MODULE 8.2

LISTENING

1 As a lead-in ask students to describe what they can see in the picture.

   Students listen to the conversation and complete the questions. You will probably have to explain the meaning of *foreman* first. In order to prepare for the speaking exercise, higher-level students should also listen for the answers to the questions. Lower-level students can do this in a second listening if it is too challenging for them.

2 Students listen again and check the things that have been done and put a cross next to the things that have not been done.

SPEAKING

1 Circulate and monitor for the correct verb forms and for pronunciation. You may need to point out that the contracted form *haven't / hasn't* is used in short answers, but *have / has* remains uncontracted in short answers.

2 You may need to explain some vocabulary here, e.g. *plumber, install, hang, put in*. Start by modeling the example question and answer, including the natural contracted forms *they've* and *they haven't*. Monitor carefully as students ask and answer the questions. Students may have difficulties with pronunciation, past participle forms, and the use of *yet*. You may like to collect mistakes you hear and put them on the board for a correction slot following the exercise.

MODULE 8.3

SPEAKING

Make sure that Student B turns immediately to page 93 and does not look at the Student A page. Give students a few minutes to read the instructions for (a) and for Student B to read the 'Things to do today' list.

Demonstrate what to do by asking the first question yourself: *Have you reserved a meeting room yet?* and getting the B students to answer *Yes, I have. I've reserved room 302.*

Circulate and check that students are using the correct verb forms and the correct word order in the questions. When they are ready, students change roles and do (b).

Students should check answers at the end of the activity by repeating the information back to their partners, e.g. *So you've reserved a meeting room; it's room 302. You've sent out an announcement; you sent it by e-mail. You're making copies of the handouts now.* etc.

MODULE 8.4

SPEAKING

Have students describe the pictures and speculate as to where they might be. They then discuss the questions in pairs / small groups. If students are stuck for ideas in (c) and (d) you can give them some prompts, e.g. ask them to think about *cost, convenience, privacy, variety, security, services*. Gather feedback at the end of their discussions and compare answers as a class.

LISTENING

You may like to start with a gist listening task by having students listen with their books closed and asking them to listen for what kind of company is being talked about.

1 Give students time to read the questions before listening. To check answers, ask students for the correct answer if the sentence was false.

2 Again, students will need time to read the questions before listening. You may need to explain the meanings of *raise money* and *purchase*.

Play the recording as many times as necessary. To check answers you can have students raise their hands / call out when they hear the answer, so that you pause the recording at the appropriate places.

You could round off the activity by asking students in which of the places mentioned they'd most like to have a holiday home and why.

MODULE 8.5

LISTENING

Give students time to look at the information and complete the conversation. Play the recording in order to check answers. You could mention that we might also naturally say *at the moment* instead of *now*. Draw students' attention to the different tenses used in the answers. Have students practice the conversation in pairs in preparation for the next activity.

SPEAKING

Have Student B turn immediately to page 94 so that they don't see Student A's information. While students are asking and answering the questions in pairs, monitor and pay particular attention to the use of the correct verb tenses.

To personalize the activity you could have students ask and answer questions about a project in their workplace / school.

MODULE 8.6

SPEAKING

Read the instructions aloud. If necessary, explain *itinerary* (a plan or route for a trip). Say the names of the cities on the map aloud to model correct pronunciation.

a Have students mark their itinerary in pencil so they can erase it later and use the map again. Circulate and make sure that students complete the correct map in the correct way. Make sure all students have completed their itinerary before they begin asking and answering questions.

b If students are not confident about the past time expressions, refer back to the Student Book, Unit 3, page 19, and use the calendar in 3.2 to practice these expressions.

Students can take turns asking questions or Student A can ask questions until he / she figures out B's itinerary, and then B asks questions. Circulate and help, checking that students answer in complete sentences using the target language. To add a competitive element, see which student can discover the other's itinerary first (if students are taking turns) or in the fewest number of turns (if Student A asks first).

c Have students compare books as a final check.

For further practice, have students change partners and repeat the whole activity.

MODULE 8.7

READING

As a lead-in you could elicit different ways companies hire new staff.

Ask four students to read the texts aloud or give students time to read them silently. Answer vocabulary questions or let students consult a dictionary. To give an objective to the reading you could ask students to find how many different hiring procedures are mentioned.

SPEAKING

1 Have someone in each group take notes on the discussion to report back later to the whole class. Encourage groups to think of an advantage and a disadvantage for each type of hiring procedure if they can.

POSSIBLE ANSWERS

1 Advantages: employees will feel loyal to the company; the company can train employees to suit its requirements.

   Disadvantages: employees have no other work experience to bring to the company; it may be difficult for employees to change jobs.

2 Advantages: the company gets people with new ideas and different experience; employees can find a new job more easily.

   Disadvantages: the company cannot expect employee loyalty or continuity; the employee cannot expect job security.

3 Advantages: the company can hire workers at a low salary and train them; employees can get a job without previous experience.

   Disadvantages: the company may not get employees with relevant experience; the employees' salary may be very low.

4 Advantages: the company can hire people who fit into the company; employees will get on with each other more easily.

   Disadvantages: the tests may not be accurate or reliable.

2   Ask students to recall their own experiences of being hired. If your students are not in full-time employment, ask them to recall their experiences in getting a part-time or vacation job or talk about people they know.

For further practice ask *If you were in charge of hiring, how would you choose employees for a restaurant / factory / small office / construction crew / elementary school / bank?*

EXTRA ACTIVITY

Have you … yet?

Use photocopiable page H, page 60. Copy and make one set of cards for each group of 3–4 students. Each group will also need a coin to toss. In order to make sure that students understand how to play the game, you should demonstrate it with them first.

Instructions for the game

1   The background to the game is that students are preparing to go on a business trip and are checking what they have / haven't done yet. The winner is the person with the fewest cards at the end of the game.

2   Students put the stack of cards face down on the table between them.

3   The first player takes the top card, and using the cue on the card, makes a *Have you … yet?* question for the student on their left. For example, if the card says *send / report / Mr Smith* the student asks the question *Have you sent the report to Mr. Smith yet?*

4   If the student makes an incorrect question, e.g. *Have you send the report to Mr. Smith yet?*, he / she must keep the card, and the next student takes a turn. (Students may ask you to judge if a question is correct or not.)

5   If the student makes a correct question, the student on their left tosses a coin. If it lands on "heads", he / she answers *Yes, I have,* the card is put to one side out of the game, and he / she picks up a new card and makes a question for the next player.

If the coin lands on "tails", he / she answers *No, I haven't* and has to supply an excuse why not, e.g. *my e-mail system isn't working.* The other students in the group decide if the excuse is valid or not. If it is, the card is put to one side out of the game. If it isn't, the student must keep the card. Students are not allowed to give an excuse that has already been given, and are not allowed to say they didn't have time. Students may ask you to judge if an excuse is valid or not, but try to encourage them to reach a decision in their group.

6   Play continues until there are no more cards left in the stack. Students then count who has the fewest cards in their hand.

9 Future prospects

REVIEW

Present perfect

Write on the board:

A *Have you* _____ *yet?*

B *Yes, I have. / No, I haven't.*

Ask students to write three questions using the present perfect and *yet*. They should then ask three different students their questions, and write down the answers. Then ask students to present information about their classmates, e.g. *Yoshi hasn't been to Singapore yet. Ms. Shabat has eaten Thai food.* Ask the B students for extra information, where possible, e.g. *I ate Thai food last weekend.*

MODULE 9.1

SPEAKING

Ask *What can you see in the picture? Where do you think the picture was taken? What is the robot doing? Do you think we will have robots serving us drinks in the future?* to lead in to the topic of forecasting and predicting.

LISTENING

1   As students have already practiced describing graphs in Unit 4, you can ask them to describe the graphs as a lead-in. However, you may need to introduce the words *unstable* and *fluctuate* for the third graph. Play the recording as many times as necessary.

2   Have students read the sentences first. With higher-level groups you can ask students to choose True or False before listening, based on what they heard in the first listening. Check answers by having students read out the true sentences and correct the sentences which are false. For further comprehension practice you can also ask what reasons Professor King gave for her forecasts.

MODULE 9.2

LISTENING

To introduce the topic ask students what kind of cars they think people will drive in the future and what will be important when choosing a car. Have students look at the pictures and crucial factors and check that they understand *investment*, CO_2 *emissions*, and *SUV* (sports utility vehicle). Play the conversation and have students follow in their books. Check understanding of *consume, emit*, and *demand*. As a follow-up you can ask students if they agree or disagree with the prediction.

SPEAKING

1   Students practice the conversation in pairs. With classes with weaker pronunciation you may like to practice as a choral drill first of all.

2   In pairs students look at the pictures and the crucial factors in the travel industry and the energy industry. Gather feedback and check understanding of *convenience, pollution*, and *renewable*. Draw students' attention to the Useful phrases by having them read them out. Monitor carefully as students ask and answer the questions. Pay attention to the use of the useful phrases given and other future forms.

3   For further practice students can change partners, or get together with another pair and compare answers. Round off the activity by gathering feedback as a class. To personalize the activity you could ask students to think about future trends in the industries in which they work.

MODULE 9.3

READING

1   Give students time to read the sentences and ask you for clarification of anything unclear. Students can do the matching exercise in pairs. Check answers by having one student read out Sentence A and another student read out the matching Sentence B.

Highlight the contracted *I'll* and drill if necessary.

Point out the use of *will* for instant or spontaneous decisions. You could clarify this by contrasting it with *going to* and present continuous for future plans. Show students an appointment in your diary and model the appropriate sentence, e.g. *I'm meeting Jane on Monday evening / I'm going to meet Jane on Monday evening.* Contrast with the sentences here. Ask concept checking questions, e.g. *In the first exchange, has B planned to have a cup of coffee?*

2   Monitor as students practice the exchanges and check for problems with pronunciation, especially question intonation and the contracted *will*.

SPEAKING

1   Give students time to look at the pictures and sentences. Then ask *Where are they? What's the situation?* You may need to explain *pick you up.* Ask students to match the photos to the sentences.

2   Elicit possible responses for the first situation, e.g. *I'll walk / take a bus / phone a cab / call my boss to say I'll be late.* Highlight the use of *will* in the responses. Students work in pairs to practice the sentences and think of appropriate responses. You could also do this as a whole-class mingling exercise, instructing students that they shouldn't give the same response twice.

MODULE 9.4

LISTENING

You can lead in by asking what a financial advisor does and by asking students if they think the airline industry is a good investment.

1   You could have students listen for gist first by asking them to keep their books closed and asking them to listen for whether the financial advisor suggests buying or selling shares in each of the two companies. Model the correct pronunciation of the phrases. Then give students time to read the sentences, before listening and filling the blanks. Check answers by having students read out the completed sentences. To avoid overload with lower-level groups, break the listening into two sections, the first about the airline and the second about the pharmaceuticals company and listen one stage at a time.

2   Check understanding of phrases and model their pronunciation. Check answers by having students read out the completed sentences.

3   Try to elicit the answer from students. If they are stuck, ask a prompting question: *In which section does he give his personal opinion?*

SPEAKING

1   Students mark their answers individually.

2   In preparation for this you may like to take the first sentence as an example and ask students to modify it using all the expressions from Listening. Draw students' attention to the position of the word or phrase in the sentence. Ask them to try to formulate a rule, i.e. expressions like *I'm sure that* go at the beginning of a sentence; adverbs like *probably* go between *will* and the main verb; modals like *might* replace *will* and go before the verb. Point out that other positions are possible but that these are the most common. Write up the sentences on the board. You can use percentages to clarify the meanings.

Students practice asking and answering the questions in pairs or small groups. Monitor for the correct expressions of possibility and future forms. Encourage students to give reasons for their opinions as much as possible.

MODULE 9.5

READING

Give students time to read through the exercise and check the boxes. Answer any vocabulary questions or let students consult a dictionary.

SPEAKING

1   Students compare answers in pairs or small groups. Make sure that they don't look at each other's books but give their opinions instead.

2   Have two students read out the example exchange. Students could also work in small groups for the discussion. Encourage them to give reasons for their opinions and to ask others for their reasons, e.g. *Oh? Why do you think so?* or *What makes you think that?* Point out that when asking a question about someone's opinion, they should try to sound curious and not challenging or disbelieving. Higher-level groups could also discuss how these

changes would affect them / their country / the world. Monitor and check for the correct future expressions. Students may have difficulties with word order.

3 Have two students read out the example exchange. You may like to demonstrate another question first by asking a student to ask you one of the questions. While students are asking and answering, circulate, again paying attention to the future forms / expressions. For further practice have students write 2–3 more questions to ask their partner. They could also swap partners / groups and do the activity again. To round off the activity collect feedback.

MODULE 9.6

SPEAKING

Student A is an investor and Student B is a financial advisor giving Student A advice on which companies to invest in.

Give students time to read the instructions and their information. Ask questions to check that they understand what to do, e.g. *Who is Student A / B? How much money does Student A have? Who is giving advice?* Deal with any vocabulary issues. Students can use calculators to help calculate how many shares to buy. Both students should write down the number of shares that Student A decides to buy in their table.

As students do the activity, circulate and listen out for problems. Pay attention to the forms used to express future possibility and give advice.

When they have finished, students should look at the share prices for the following year and calculate how much money the investor has made or lost. You can get feedback from each pair to see who was the most successful.

For further discussion, you can ask students if they had $10,000 to invest in shares, which real company they would invest in and why.

MODULE 9.7

READING

Give students time to read the statements and make sure they understand them. Answer any vocabulary questions or let students consult a dictionary.

SPEAKING

1 In multilingual classes, students from different countries could work together and compare answers.

2 Be prepared to offer information about other countries in case your students don't have any ideas, e.g. in Korea and Japan, most company employees receive a bonus twice a year; in the UK most banks offer a free overdraft service, up to a certain limit, and millions of people participate in the twice-weekly national lottery game.

For further practice, present these discussion questions about money, and / or ask students to suggest their own discussion questions.

In your country:

Do children receive an allowance from their parents? At what age and how much?

Is the husband or wife responsible for the family budget?

Do most people use department store or other similar credit cards for shopping?

What kinds of special offers do credit card companies use to win customers, e.g. airline mileage, extended warranties, rebates, special gifts, etc.?

EXTRA ACTIVITY

In 30 years ...

Use photocopiable page I, page 61. Copy and cut out the cards, giving one to each student. In smaller classes, use only some of the conversations.

Write on the board *In 30 years ...* and tell students that on their card they have a sentence from a three-line conversation about the future. They should mingle, tell their sentence to the other students, and try to find the two people who have the other two sentences from their conversation. When they have found the other members of their group, they should sit down together.

Encourage students to look at their card as little as possible during the mingling exercise. If you have a higher-level class, you could have them memorize their sentence and mingle without using their card. As students mingle, circulate and check that they are forming the correct groups.

When students are sitting in groups, have them read out their conversation. They should continue to discuss the topic of their conversation, giving their own opinions.

For further practice, you can write the topics on the board as students read out their conversation, and have the groups discuss all the topics.

If you have fewer than six students, instead of mingling, put students in pairs and give each pair the complete set of sentences. They should arrange them into five conversations, and then discuss the topics.

10 Regulations and advice

REVIEW

Making predictions

Write on the board:

A *What do you think you'll do this evening / this weekend / on your next vacation, etc.?*

B *I'm not sure but I'll probably / I might _____.*

Students ask and answer questions in pairs. Their answers need not be true. As a follow-up, have each pair get together with another pair to share information, e.g. *Next weekend, Mr. _____ will probably visit some old friends. / He might play golf,* etc.

MODULE 10.1

SPEAKING

Ask *Where is he? What's his job? What qualifications / qualities do you need to do this job?*

LISTENING

1 Have students read the instructions and the job information. Before students listen, put them in pairs to try to guess where the mistakes are. Then play the recording and do the exercises.

2 Pause the recording after the missing information to allow students enough time to write in their answers.

Highlight the short answer forms as students may tend to say *Yes, you have / No, you haven't.*

SPEAKING

Model the correct pronunciation of *have to* (/hæf tə/) and *has to* (/hæs tə/), and contrast them with *have* (/hæv/) and *has* (/hæz/). For further practice do a memory quiz. Student A closes the book and Student B asks *Do you have to ...* questions. Student A answers *Yes, you do. / No, you don't.* Then repeat the exercise with Student A asking the questions.

To personalize the activity you can have students make sentences about the qualities needed to do their jobs.

MODULE 10.2

READING

Before starting this section, review the meaning of the four modals, i.e. *have to = it's necessary to; don't have to = it's not necessary to; can = it's possible / permissible; can't = it's not possible / not allowed.* Write the modals and their meanings on the board for students to refer to.

1 Students work alone or in pairs. Check answers by asking *Which sentence goes with picture 1 / 2 / 3 / 4?*

2 Put students in pairs to do the exercise.

3 If two students have different answers, they can check with another pair or with you. Finally, check the answers with the whole class.

SPEAKING

Do this exercise in pairs or as a whole-class activity. With higher-level classes have students close their books and answer the questions from memory. If students are working in pairs, circulate to help and monitor correct pronunciation of *have to* (/hæf tə/).

For further practice ask students to underline all the words and phrases in this section that are typically used in connection with airline travel, e.g. *boarding pass, get on the plane, fasten your seatbelt, stow your luggage,* etc. Have students brainstorm other words and phrases related to air travel, and write them on the board, e.g. *check in, reconfirm your flight, departure lounge, delayed / canceled flight, customs,* etc. To practice the vocabulary, put students in groups of four or five, and have one or two students act out a short skit about some stage of air travel, while the other students guess what they are doing, e.g. *You're checking your luggage. You're picking up your carry-on bag. You're going to the departure lounge,* etc.

MODULE 10.3

READING

Students work in pairs. Check answers by asking students to make sentences such as *A hospital doctor has to keep his / her beeper switched on at all times.* Remind students of the correct pronunciation of *has to* (/hæs tə/). For further practice, have students brainstorm additional regulations for each of the six jobs.

SPEAKING

1 Circulate to make sure students choose a company quickly, and spend most of their time making a list of regulations. Help with vocabulary, if necessary, or encourage students to use a dictionary. If some students finish early, have them choose a second company and make another list.

2 If your class is small enough, pairs could present their regulations to the whole class. This activity could also be done in a "Twenty Questions" format, i.e. the class asks a pair of students a maximum of twenty *yes / no* questions about regulations to try to find out the type of company, e.g. *Do you have to work overtime? Do you have to wear a uniform? Can you smoke during working hours? Do you have to speak a foreign language?* etc.

WRITING

Have students make lists individually first, and then talk about them in groups of three or four. Circulate and help if necessary, and check that students use the target modal structures correctly.

MODULE 10.4

LISTENING

Before they listen have students brainstorm the following question: *What kind of advice would you give someone about to take a long flight?* Write their ideas on the board.

1 When students have finished matching, ask them to give advice using the words to check understanding.

2 You may like to have students predict the answers, before listening again to check.

SPEAKING

1 As further practice, have students ask each other questions, e.g. *Is it a good idea to _____? Should I _____? Do you think I should _____?*

2 Be ready to provide some additional ideas yourself, e.g. *wear comfortable shoes, use a sleep mask, set your watch to the time zone of your destination before you depart,* etc.

For further practice ask students to give advice on other aspects of travel, e.g. *buying a ticket, packing, choosing a hotel, carrying money, buying souvenirs,* etc.

EXTRA ACTIVITY

More ways of giving advice

Elicit from the class or present additional modals for giving advice and write them in a list on the board, with the most tentative at the top and the strongest at the bottom, e.g. *could, ought to, need to, had better, must.*

Note: Some learners frequently underestimate the strength of *had better*, which implies a consequence, e.g. *You had better get to work on time or you'll get in trouble.* You may need to spend some time practicing this and monitoring its use in subsequent activities.

You can also include expressions like *If I were you, I would / wouldn't _____ / Try _____ing / Why don't you _____?* Give example sentences with each expression, or elicit examples from the class.

Students can use these additional modals to make sentences about the advice in this unit or in photocopiable activity J on page 62 (see page 45 for teaching notes).

MODULE 10.5

WRITING

Students look at the photo. Ask *What are the three people doing? What do you think they are saying?*

Ensure that students write their advice in complete sentences, using a modal expression. If any students finish early, they can write down more than one idea for some of the problems.

SPEAKING

1   Put students into groups of three to five. Circulate and make sure they use the target language correctly.

To extend the activity, form larger groups and have students pretend that they work in the sales division and are having a meeting with the manager to discuss the problems. They should suggest solutions using the expressions in 10.4 Speaking 1 and in the Extra activity above. After listening to all the ideas, the group can choose the one they like the best.

2   If students do not have a problem that they wish to share, they can invent one. Write some language on the board for accepting advice, e.g. *Thanks, that's a good idea. / Thank you, I'll try that. / That's a good suggestion.* Point out that it's polite to thank someone for advice, even if you do not intend to follow it.

EXTRA ACTIVITY

Suggestion box

1   Prepare some problem situations in advance, if possible ones related to your students' work lives, e.g. *I feel too tired to work in the afternoons. / My assistant doesn't work very efficiently. / I made a big mistake on the report I turned in. / I lost my customer's phone number,* etc.

2   Give each student a number of small slips of paper or index cards. Then read one problem aloud. Students should write one suggestion or piece of advice on a slip of paper and give it to you. Paperclip the suggestions to the problem. Repeat this procedure for each problem.

3   Read each problem with all the accompanying suggestions aloud. Have the class vote on the one they like best. The student whose advice is chosen gets one point. The student with the most points at the end of the activity is the winner.

As a variation, and if you have access to English-language advice columns, read some letters aloud to the class, and have them write their own replies on a slip of paper as described above. Then re-read the letter, the students' advice, and the original answer in the advice column. See if any student gave the same advice or if anyone gave better advice!

MODULE 10.6

READING

Read the texts aloud, have students read them aloud, or let students read them silently. Students may have more than one idea about what the mistake is. Encourage them to write down all their ideas.

SPEAKING

1   Students can work in pairs or small groups. Encourage them to use the expressions practiced in the unit in their answers, e.g. *I don't think she should begin talking about business right away. In Brazil, you have to spend some time making small talk before you talk about business,* etc. Have one student in each group make notes about the group's ideas to report back to the whole class.

2   In multilingual classes you could have students from the same country working together. Be ready to offer prompts if they don't have ideas, e.g. ask them about attitudes to time, ways of addressing each other, levels of formality, mixing business and socializing. Higher-level groups could write a short skit about someone making a cultural mistake, and perform it for the class. In this way they can also demonstrate inappropriate body language or gestures.

EXTRA ACTIVITY

Advice role play cards

1   Use photocopiable page J, page 62. Students work in pairs or small groups. Photocopy enough sets of the cards for each pair or group to have three or four cards at one time. When they finish with their cards, they pass them on to another group.

2   Students place the cards face down in a stack. Student A picks up a card and reads the situation aloud, and the other student(s) give advice. Lower-level students can refer to their books for the target language. Student A should make a response to the suggestions, e.g. *That's a good idea. / What a good suggestion.* Encourage students to give as many suggestions as possible. When the other student(s) cannot think of any more suggestions, Student B picks up the next card, reads it aloud, and the procedure is repeated.

3   To extend the activity, higher-level students could write a short skit based on one of the situations on the role cards and perform it for the class.

REVIEW

Offering advice

Write on the board:

1   I lost my train pass.
2   I forgot my e-mail password.
3   I promised two different colleagues I'd have dinner with them tonight.
4   Your own idea.

Students work in pairs and take turns giving a problem and offering advice.

MODULE 11.1

SPEAKING

Ask *Who are they? Where are they? What are they doing? Do you often go to meetings? What kinds of meetings? Do you like meetings?*

LISTENING

1   To lead in to the listening, ask students *What do you know about Australia / Australian products? What Australian products are popular in your country? Why do people attend product fairs? Why do organizations host product fairs?*

Read the instructions before playing the recording and having students do the exercise. Play the recording again, and have students write down a few words that indicate which topics are being discussed, e.g. *folk band, live music* for 'music'; *cooking demonstrations, wine tasting* for 'food and drink', etc. Check the answers and ask *How do you know they were talking about art / music?* etc.

2   Have students read the expressions first. Then play the recording. Check answers by asking *Which expression did you hear first / second / third?* etc. Ask students *When do we use these expressions?* to elicit answers like *to make a suggestion / ask for a suggestion / agree / disagree.*

MODULE 11.2

LISTENING

Elicit from students or explain the meaning of *promotion* (advertising or another activity intended to increase sales or make something well known) and *run an ad* (to publish / put an ad in a newspaper or magazine). Read the instructions and play the recording. Ask *Which speaker is in charge of the meeting?* (Speaker A); *How do you know?* (She begins the meeting, asks for suggestions, and decides to discuss the details later).

Point out that in English-speaking countries the chair of a meeting is usually responsible for beginning and ending the meeting, following the agenda, and getting ideas from the participants, as well as giving his / her own ideas. Other members may give ideas, ask questions, and agree or disagree with ideas. Ask *Are these roles different in your country?* (possible differences: a secretary is responsible for the agenda; the chair presents most ideas; other participants, especially if they are lower-ranking, do not openly disagree or present new ideas). Teach *to brainstorm* (generate ideas through discussion). Ask *In your country are ideas generated before meetings or during meetings?*

SPEAKING

1   If students do not divide evenly, one student could read both B and D. Have students role-play the meeting: Student A should sit at the head of the table; participants should take notes on the ideas presented, without referring to the notes in the book, if possible.

2   Encourage students to hold the "meeting" and just look at the prompts, without reading the entire script of the conversation in the Listening script.

3   Have students form new groups. Give them a few minutes to think of ideas. Circulate and help with vocabulary and suggestions if students cannot think of their own idea for the final part of the exercise, e.g. decide where to go on vacation; design a new company brochure. When students have finished, have groups present one discussion to the whole class.

MODULE 11.3

SPEAKING

As a lead-in ask *Do you / your friends ever shop in shopping malls? What kinds of shops are there? What kinds of things do you like to buy there?*

1 Students first work alone. They should also write down the reasons for their choices. Have students read the Useful language and quiz them by having them cover their books while you ask *What can I say to give an opinion / ask someone else for an idea / agree / disagree?* Then put students in groups of three or four to discuss their plan, using the conversation pattern in 11.2. One student should chair the meeting. Encourage students to come to a consensus.

2 If your class is not too large, have each group make a brief presentation to the class on their plan and how they chose it. Students could also write a short paragraph explaining which stores they chose and why.

EXTRA ACTIVITY

Planning for visitors

1 Use photocopiable page K, page 63. Make one copy for each group of three or four students.

2 Tell students that they are going to have a meeting to organize the visit of two important guests. Students are representatives of a tool company and the visitors are from ElectroCraft and are visiting to see if they can outsource some of their electronic tools productions to the students' company. They should work together to decide on the points on the agenda, e.g. *Where will the visitors stay? Who will book it? Who will meet them at the airport?* etc. If necessary, have students review the language presented in 11.1 and 11.2 before they begin. Assign each student a role to play from the people attending (Managing Director, Production Director, etc.). If you have groups of three you can leave out one of the roles. Have students read through the agenda first and ask some checking questions to make sure that everything is clear, e.g. *Why are the visitors coming? What does 'accommodation' mean? What is R&D? What different kinds of entertainment can you think of?*

3 When students have finished, put two groups together to explain their plan to each other.

If students are from the same company, they can make plans for visitors (real or imagined) to their own company.

MODULE 11.4

LISTENING

1 Read the instructions. Students work alone or in pairs to match the definitions. Check answers by asking *What does "a search facility" mean?* etc.

2 Read the instructions and the headings in the chart. For each heading ask *What kinds of ideas do you think they're going to discuss?* Students should write notes, not complete sentences. With lower-level classes, have one or two students take notes on each topic; next have them share their notes in groups before listening again to the whole conversation. Then put students in groups of three and have them check their answers by looking at the listening script in the back of the Student Book. Students can also practice the conversation. Circulate and assist with pronunciation and intonation.

SPEAKING

Put students in pairs or small groups to discuss the questions. Assign one person in each pair / group to write down the ideas and report them to the whole class. If you have computer access, students can show each other their favorite website or company website (if they are from different companies).

If students are from the same company, you can have them discuss the strengths and weaknesses of their website and ideas for improving it.

EXTRA ACTIVITY

Designing a website

1 Students work in groups of three. If the groups are not the same as those that discussed the questions in 11.4, give them a few minutes to talk about websites they like and don't like.

2 Give out blank sheets of paper and colored pens. Tell students that they are going to design their own website. Let them choose their own

purpose for the website or offer ideas, e.g. *your English class; a hobby or interest all group members have in common; an invented company; a product or service; a familiar location.* Students can create "links" by using additional sheets of paper; they should have a "button" on the first page (the "home page"), indicating that there is further information. Allow plenty of time (at least 20–30 minutes) and encourage students to be creative!

3   When students have finished, put two groups together to share their creations. Group members can either explain their website and its features or the other group can ask questions and follow the "links" to see where they lead. When the demonstrations are over, ask each group to describe three things they liked about the other group's website.

MODULE 11.5

SPEAKING

Note: In many graduate business programs around the world, analysing case studies is a popular form of instruction with which students are expected to be familiar. This activity is a simple way of introducing case studies. Explain briefly what is involved: students have some information to read and a problem to solve. The problem-solving often involves group discussions and decision-making, and students should be able to justify their decisions.

1   Put students in groups of three or four to discuss the cases. Circulate to help with vocabulary, if necessary, or encourage students to consult a dictionary. Lower-level classes may find the vocabulary level in this section quite high. You may need to pre-teach some of the vocabulary.

Students should make notes about the reasons for their choices. They can refer back to 11.1 and 11.2 for expressions to use during their discussion.

2   After groups have reached a consensus have the whole class vote to find out the most popular options.

There are no right or wrong solutions to the case studies but you might want to talk through these suggestions with the class once they have finished.

Case Study 1

Option A: A conservative decision. OK, but it won't help your company expand.

Option B: 'Sequenced entry'. This is the best way to enter a new business. If you are successful, you can expand. If you fail, you don't lose much.

Option C: Risky. You could lose a lot of money.

Case Study 2

Option A: A good decision. It is easier to expand capacity if there is an increasing demand for a product or service.

Option B: Dangerous. Your decision could lead to overcapacity, price cuts, and reduced profit.

Option C: A common mistake. If previous efforts to help a weak company have failed, more money won't help.

In order to reduce overload it's a good idea to do the case studies one at a time.

For further practice with higher-level classes, ask students to write their own case study for homework. They could base the case study on a business decision in their own company, or a company they know about. Stress that students must choose decisions that have already been made and not problems currently under consideration. They must identify the problem or choice that had to be made; list two or three options; indicate which option was chosen; and evaluate whether that option was a good choice or not. Then in class students present their case studies to the whole class or in small groups. The other students say which option they prefer and why. The presenter then explains the choice the company made and why, and what happened as a result.

MODULE 11.6

READING

1   To set the scene ask some or all of the following questions: *What does "negotiating" mean? What are some situations when you must negotiate? What qualities does a good negotiator have? Do you think negotiating styles are different in different countries? Do you know about any different negotiating styles? When people from two different nationalities do*

business, whose negotiating style should be used: the customer's or the host's?

Choose a student to read each paragraph aloud. Ask the whole class or put students in groups to discuss these questions: *Which of these styles are similar to negotiating styles in your country? Which styles are different? If any are different, would they be easy or challenging for you to adapt to?*

2   Go through the questions to check understanding.

SPEAKING

1   In multilingual classes, students of the same nationality could work together, but this is not essential. If groups don't know what kind of advice to offer, ask questions to prompt them, e.g. *Is a good negotiator in your country direct or indirect, formal or informal? Are negotiations long and detailed or brief? Where and when do people meet to negotiate,* e.g. *at the office, during meals, in the evenings, on weekends?* etc.

2   Have each group choose a spokesperson to present the group's advice to the class. In multilingual classes let each student talk briefly about negotiating styles in his / her country. Summarize key information about each country on the board while students are speaking.

12 Speaking in public

REVIEW

Making suggestions

Write on the board:

1 *Plan the annual company picnic.*

2 *Plan an evening out in your town for foreign visitors.*

3 *Choose a gift for your manager who's retiring.*

4 *Think of a fun way to practice English.*

Students work in groups of four or five. Each group chooses one situation and students make suggestions. One person in each group should write down the suggestions to report to the class.

MODULE 12.1

SPEAKING

Ask about the photo *What is the man in the middle doing? Do you ever make presentations or attend presentations? Are they formal or informal? How formal do you think the presentation in the picture is? Who do you think he is presenting to?*

LISTENING

To introduce the topic elicit tips for giving successful presentations.

1 Give students time to read the exercise first. Check answers by asking *What did she talk about first / second?* etc. You can also ask students if she included the same tips as they gave for giving successful presentations.

2 Pause the recording if necessary to give students time to write in their answers. You may like to point out at this stage that it is conventional to outline the structure of your presentation at the beginning and that this also helps the listeners to follow you.

MODULE 12.2

READING

Give students time to read the information and ask you about anything unclear. You may like to model and drill the useful expressions in order

work on pronunciation and to help students feel comfortable using them.

SPEAKING

Students give their presentation to their partner first of all. Monitor and give help where necessary. You could ask partners to make comments on what their partners did well / not so well in their presentation, if group dynamics allow.

Afterwards students can present to the group. Have them stand up and present at the front of the class to make the experience more realistic.

For further practice you can have students give short presentations on a topic of their own choosing, e.g. something connected with their work, a hobby, or a travel experience. Students can prepare for homework, using the same framework, and present in the following class.

MODULE 12.3

LISTENING

You could start with a gist listening activity by having students listen to the recording with their books closed and answer the question *What is the purpose of the speech?*

1 Give students time to read the exercise first. You may well need to explain the meaning of *propose a toast.* Check answers by asking *What did Barry say first / second, etc?*

2 With higher-level groups you could have students predict the answers before listening and then listen again to check. Check answers by having students read out the complete sentences.

You may need to explain *appreciate* and *look forward to.*

MODULE 12.4

READING

1 Before students read the extracts, ask *What kinds of things could you mention during a speech for each of these occasions?* Accept any reasonable answers. Then have students work alone or in

pairs to match the speeches with the events. Circulate and answer any vocabulary questions. Check answers by saying the subject of the speech and asking a student to give the number of the speech.

2 Students work alone and check their answers in pairs. Then check answers as a group.

SPEAKING

Put students in groups to give the speeches. Encourage them to add extra details to their speech. Remind students to sound enthusiastic and make eye contact during the speech. You could also ask students to include a toast at the end of their speech, reminding them of the form *To … .* If toasts are included, they should mime raising glasses for the toast.

For further practice have students work in pairs and prepare a speech for one of the following situations: welcome a new colleague; congratulate a colleague on his / her engagement / marriage; an end-of-year office party; the announcement of a new project / joint venture; congratulate a colleague on the successful completion of a training course. Students may make brief notes to refer to but should look at the audience as much as possible during the speech.

MODULE 12.5

SPEAKING

1 Students work in pairs / small groups to prepare their speech using the instructions. Make sure that they write notes and not the whole speech out in full. If you think students may have trouble coming up with ideas, you can brainstorm the different sections as a class first and write up ideas on the board. While students are preparing, circulate and help with ideas or vocabulary as necessary.

2 If time allows, one person from each pair / group should give their speech to the class. You could make this into a party by bringing in some snacks and drinks, if appropriate.

EXTRA ACTIVITY

Thank you, everyone

1 Write on the board:
   A *Goodbye, (name). Thank you for _____ .*
   B *Goodbye, (name). Thank you for _____. I hope to see you again sometime.*

2 Tell students to stand up, and say goodbye and thank you to each student in the class. Before they begin, give some examples of things they can thank classmates for, e.g. helping me with my English; being my partner; having a good sense of humor; being a lively student; asking interesting questions. Students should shake hands as they speak. Include yourself in the exercise.

MODULE 12.6

READING

Ask *What does 'client care' mean? Why is client care important? How can it help your business?* Accept any reasonable answers, e.g. *It improves the company's image, increases customer loyalty, adds a personal touch,* etc.

Read the list aloud or give students time to read it to themselves.

SPEAKING

Have someone in each group record ideas to share with the whole class. Make a list on the board of methods used in the countries / companies represented in your class. For further practice have students rank the items in the list from the most important to the least important.

To extend the discussion ask the following questions: *Are any methods of client care appropriate / not appropriate in your country?* (in some countries expensive gifts may be given; in other countries companies have strict policies against accepting or giving expensive gifts). *If you were a client, which kinds of care would please you the most? What are some drawbacks to this kind of client care?* (expense; time; some customers might feel pressured).

EXTRA ACTIVITY

Tic tac toe

This activity reviews the language practiced throughout the Student Book.

1 Use photocopiable page L, page 64.

2 For the first game, use Set 1. Play in groups of three or four. Decide who is the leader and who are the players in each group. Give the leader the Set 1 answer sheet, and tell him / her not to show it to the other players.

3 Draw this grid on the board:

1	2	3
4	5	6
7	8	9

Have the leader copy it onto a sheet of paper.

4 Student A starts by choosing a square in the grid, and telling the leader the number of the square. The leader reads out the corresponding answer from Set 1, and Student A must provide a question or answer to match it. (There may be more than one possible response.) If Student A gives an acceptable response, he / she "takes" the square by marking it with his / her initials. Student B goes next, and so on.

If a student gets the response wrong or cannot think of a suitable response, the square remains open for other students to choose.

5 Circulate and help the leaders if there are any doubts about the acceptability of a response.

The first player to get three squares in a line (across, down, or diagonally) wins. If no one gets a line, the player with the most squares wins.

If you have time, play again with a different leader, using Sets 2–4.

1 You are at a conference in Hong Kong. Complete the information about yourself. **Do not** use your real name, job, etc.

Name: _____

Job: _____

Company: _____

Company information: _____

Nationality: _____

Home town: _____

Languages: _____

Hobby/ies: _____

Hotel you are staying at: _____

Length of stay: _____

---

2 Talk to as many people as you can at the conference. Remember to start and end the conversations politely!

Find the person at the conference who ...

Name:

1 has the best job. _____

2 has traveled farthest to the conference _____

3 speaks the most languages. _____

4 has the most interesting hobby. _____

5 is staying in Hong Kong the longest. _____

1A You're from United Plastics. You want to speak to Mr. Lee. You want to make an appointment to see him next week to discuss the new project.

1B You're Mr. Lee. Next week you're busy all day Monday, Tuesday morning, and all day Thursday.

2A You're from City Motors. You'd like to speak to Mr. Brown. You want to talk to him about the sales figures. Find out if he can come to your office on Friday. Leave a message if he isn't there.

2B You're a receptionist at City Motors. You take a call for Mr. Brown, but there are two Mr Browns in the company: one in Accounting and one in Sales. Ask *Do you know what department he is in?* Mr Brown in Sales isn't answering his phone. Take a message.

3A You're from Goldman and Grant. You'd like to speak to Ms. Ponti. You want to tell her that the meeting time has changed to 3:00 p.m.

3B You're Ms. Ponti's assistant. She's on another line. Ask if he / she would like to hold or leave a message.

4A You're from ABC Industries. You want to speak to Ms. Kim. If she isn't there, leave a message for her to call you. Your number is 517-335-8792.

4B You're Ms. Kim's assistant. She's out of town this week on business. Ask the caller if you can take a message.

5A You're from KMT Chemicals (Tel. 210-396-4023). You'd like to speak with Mr. Gibson. It's very important that you speak with him today.

5B You work for the Southwest Supplies. You're Mr. Gibson's assistant. He's away from his desk right now, and will be in and out all afternoon. Ask the caller if he / she would like to leave a message or call back later.

6A You're from Alpha Design. You want to tell Mr. Moore that his fax did not arrive: you received only two pages instead of three. You want to ask him to send the fax again. Your fax number is 505-983-2259.

6B You're Mr. Moore's assistant. He's in a meeting right now. You're not sure when it will end. Ask the caller if you can take a message.

	Monday	Tuesday	Wednesday	Thursday	Friday
8:30					
11:00					
1:00					
3:00					
5:00					

Make eight appointments with other students. Use the ideas below or your own ideas.

- have a breakfast meeting
- join me for lunch
- come to my office to discuss the plans
- show me how to use the new software
- discuss the project over dinner
- play a few rounds of golf
- come to lunch with our supplier
- meet after work for a few drinks

Use the conversation below to make your appointments. Write the person's name and why you are meeting in the calendar above.

A Hello, B. Can you (join me for lunch) on (Tuesday) at (1:00 p.m.)?

B Yes, that would be fine. / I'm sorry, but I'm (having a breakfast meeting with C) then. How about (Wednesday) at (1:00 p.m.)?

A OK. I'll pencil you in. B is (joining me for lunch) on (Wednesday) at (1:00 p.m.).

To change an appointment:

A I'm sorry, B, but something's come up. I'm afraid I can't make our appointment on (Tuesday). Can we reschedule for (Thursday) at (11:00 a.m.)?

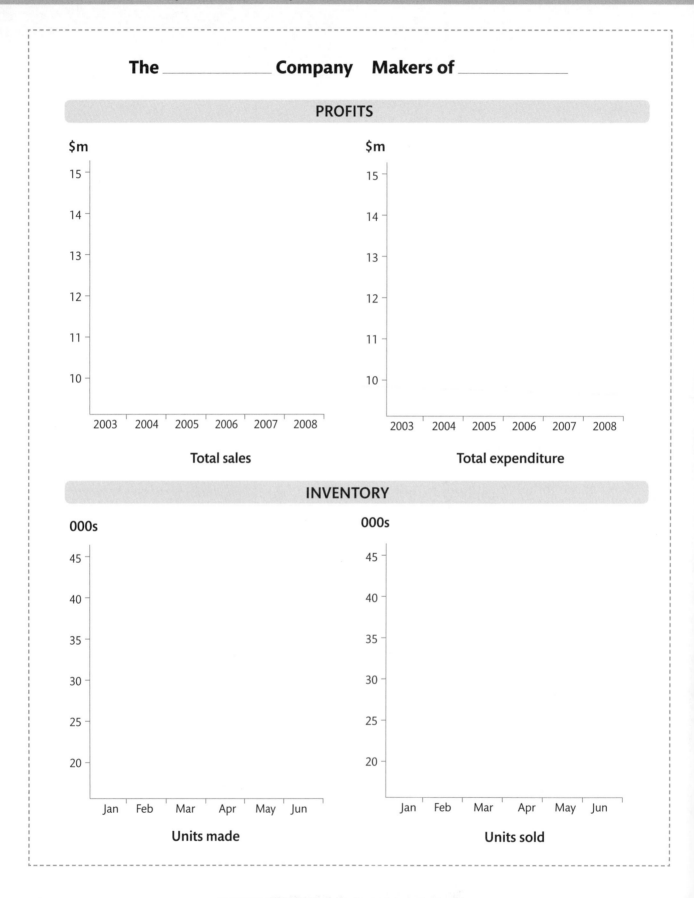

The _____ Company Makers of _____

PROFITS

$m

Total sales

$m

Total expenditure

INVENTORY

000s

Units made

000s

Units sold

Night vision binoculars

- can be used in almost total darkness
- lightweight and easy to carry
- _____
- _____
- Price _____

Garden tidy cart

- convenient
- adjustable bag height
- _____
- _____
- Price _____

CCTV home security system

- for indoor and outdoor use
- easy to install
- _____
- _____
- Price _____

Paper shredder

- compact
- easy to operate
- _____
- _____
- Price _____

Natural alarm clock

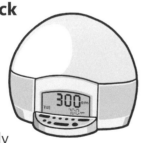

- wakes you up gently
- your own personal sunrise
- _____
- _____
- Price _____

Motorized revolving tie rack

- practical and stylish
- suitable for belts and scarves
- _____
- _____
- Price _____

Photocopiable page F Unit 6, see page 29

Jody had an idea for a new line of frozen vegetarian dishes.	Jody called her friend Jim.	Jim agreed to be Jody's partner.	They decided that Jim would create the new dishes.
They decided that Jody would take care of the business decisions.	Jim perfected the recipes.	Jody and Jim chose a name for their products.	Jody and Jim needed to find a store to carry their products.
Jody and Jim showed their products to several stores in the local shopping mall.	The mall stores didn't like the products.	A small downtown store saw the products and thought they were excellent.	The downtown store agreed to carry the products.
The products were very popular.	Other stores wanted to sell the products.	Jody and Jim made a small profit the first year.	In five years, Jody and Jim began to sell their products nationwide.

A The order hasn't arrived yet. **A** Then it should be here by Friday. <div align="right">1</div>	**B** We sent it yesterday. **B** Please let me know if it doesn't arrive. <div align="right">1</div>
A The order hasn't arrived yet. **A** Well, we never received it. <div align="right">2</div>	**B** Our records show we sent it last month. **B** All right, we'll send it again. <div align="right">2</div>
A We ordered 50 units, not 15. **A** Thank you very much. <div align="right">3</div>	**B** I'm very sorry. I'll send the rest immediately. **B** I'm sorry about the inconvenience. <div align="right">3</div>
A We ordered 15 units, not 50. **A** Will you pay for the shipping? <div align="right">4</div>	**B** Please send the rest back to us. **B** Yes, of course. <div align="right">4</div>
A The item was damaged in shipping. **A** Sure. When can we have a replacement? <div align="right">5</div>	**B** Could you return it to us? **B** I'll send one this afternoon. <div align="right">5</div>
A The item was damaged in shipping. **A** I'm afraid it's too late. Please cancel our order. <div align="right">6</div>	**B** Would you like a replacement? **B** I understand. We'll send you a refund. <div align="right">6</div>
A The item looks different from the picture in the catalogue. **A** Oh! I should have ordered a D5. <div align="right">7</div>	**B** Let's see, you ordered a B5. **B** No problem. I'll send a D5 to you today. <div align="right">7</div>
A I ordered a B5, but you sent a D5. **A** Yes, can you a B5 this week? <div align="right">8</div>	**B** I'm very sorry. Can you return the D5? **B** Yes, I'll send it tomorrow morning. <div align="right">8</div>
A We ordered black, but we received blue. **A** I guess we'll keep the blue ones, then. <div align="right">9</div>	**B** I'm afraid the black is out of stock. **B** I'm sorry about the inconvenience. <div align="right">9</div>
A We ordered blue, but we received black. **A** Yes, please. When can you do that? <div align="right">10</div>	**B** Would you like us to replace them? **B** I'll send the blue ones out this afternoon. <div align="right">10</div>

e-mail / itinerary / Mr. Song?	exchange / money?	set / out-of-office message / your computer?	arrange / meeting / Ms. Gupta?
make copies / new brochure?	write / project report?	get / visa?	book / taxi / to airport?
make / hotel reservation?	buy / flight tickets?	reserve / meeting room?	buy / gift / Mr. Simpson?
prepare / presentation?	book / rental car?	send / sales figures / Mr. Nobu?	find / good restaurant / dinner?

PHOTOCOPIABLE   © Oxford University Press

Do you think most people will live to be 100?

Maybe, people are already living longer.

But there are a lot of diseases like cancer.

Do you think most people will work at home?

Probably, because it will save companies a lot of money.

Yes, but what about people who work in shops and restaurants?

Do you think people will learn English by computer?

No, I think people prefer learning with a teacher.

You could be right, but learning by computer is cheaper.

How do you think we'll travel in the city?

I think we'll all use electric bicycles to protect the environment.

I disagree, I think we'll use electric cars.

Do you think people will read newspapers?

No, I think they'll probably read the news online.

Yes, then they won't have to buy a newspaper.

Two foreign clients are visiting your country. They want to know about some interesting things to see and do on their trip. They have two free evenings and one free weekend.	The person who sits next to you often falls asleep at his desk. He / She asks you for advice.	You and three of your friends decide to take a trip together for five days. Suggest where to go, how to get there, and what to do while you're there.
Your section needs to talk frequently with a factory in the USA. However, the time difference causes problems. Your manager wants to know if you have any suggestions about how to communicate more effectively.	A businessman is visiting your town / city with his wife and two children (8 and 10 years old). He would like suggestions for places his family could visit during the day while he is working.	Your department has some money to spend. There is enough for a new computer, a new copy machine, or one other piece of equipment. Your supervisor wants to know what you think.
Your co-worker likes her job very much, but she doesn't get along with her boss. She wants your advice.	Your company has decided to open a new branch. What city should it be in? Make some suggestions. Think carefully about a good place because you will be transferred there.	A foreign co-worker has been living in your country for six months, but hasn't made any friends yet. He / She asks for your advice about ways to meet people outside work.
Your company is asking employees to suggest ways to improve employee enthusiasm and morale.	The company cafeteria wants to improve its service, and is asking employees to make some suggestions.	Your cousin has just graduated from college, and wants your advice on how to get a good job.

Attending:	Managing Director, Sales Director, Production Director, Assistant to the MD

Meeting Agenda

Objective:	to organize the details of the visit of Mr. Cox and Ms. Ryan, from ElectroCraft Tools, Chicago.
Arrival:	16.45 Tuesday 23rd
Departure:	10.20 Thursday 25th

Details	When?	Who?
Airport pick-up		
Accommodation		
Business program		
Office visit – company presentation		
Factory visit		
R&D dept. visit		
Entertainment		
Gifts		

Set 1

1 10:30 is fine.

2 I'm very sorry about that.

3 They probably will.

4 You can use it in your car.

5 An apple juice, please.

6 I don't think I agree.

7 Yes, I have.

8 They fell slightly.

9 I'll give him your message.

Set 2

1 She's giving a presentation at 1:30.

2 They might not. I'm not sure.

3 It's the same size as a fax machine.

4 It's very interesting.

5 I haven't finished it yet.

6 I'll get you another one right away.

7 Because they wanted to increase sales.

8 We decided to start a website.

9 Yes, I did it yesterday.

Set 3

1 No problem. Go right ahead.

2 It's designed for business travelers.

3 It will be available in June.

4 No, I haven't.

5 No, thank you. I'll call back later.

6 I agree.

7 He's having lunch with a client.

8 Yes, you can.

9 Yes, I called him an hour ago.

Set 4

1 That's a good idea.

2 Not at all. I just got here.

3 We'll take care of it right away.

4 Not yet. I'm doing it now.

5 They rose sharply.

6 I'm sure it won't.

7 I'm sorry, but I'm busy then.

8 That sounds like fun.

9 About the same price as a CD player.

Tests

INTRODUCTION

There are two progress tests: Test 1 covers Units 1–6, and Test 2 covers Units 7–12. Each test has three components: a listening test, a written test, and a speaking test.

All the test material on pages 67–77 is photocopiable.

The listening and written tests have been devised so that they are quick and easy to administer. The speaking tests will take more time and effort, but where possible, they should form a part of the assessment of your students' progress. The ideas for speaking tests given below aim to provide some basic, practical techniques which take account of the real time constraints teachers face. They can, of course, be adapted to suit your teaching situation and the needs of your students.

LISTENING TESTS

Give each student a copy of the test, and allow the class a few minutes to read the instructions and the test items. Decide how many times you are going to play the recording, and tell students – for the average class, twice should be sufficient. Play the recording through from beginning to end. You may need to pause the recording between each exercise to allow students time to write, but do not pause or stop the recording during an exercise. The time needed for the listening test will vary, but on average it should take about 15–20 minutes.

Listening scripts for the listening tests are on page 78 and 79. The Answer key is on page 80. The Listening tests are on Track 53 and 54 of the Audio CD.

WRITTEN TESTS

Give each student a copy of the test. The time needed for the test may vary, but on average it should take about 20 minutes. The Answer key is on page 80.

SPEAKING TESTS

Below are three techniques for testing your students' speaking skills: interviews, role plays, and presentations. You could use one or more of these techniques, depending on the time available. Clearly, the more time you can spend on the test, the larger the sample of language you will have to assess.

A photocopiable evaluation scale is provided on page 77 to help you assess your students' speaking skills. By using this scale you can assess your students' fluency, accuracy, pronunciation, and comprehension as they progress through the course.

Equivalent number and letter grades would be:

Grade	Letter	Number
4	A	75–100
3	B	60–74
2	C	50–59
1	D	49 and below

The evaluation scale is the same as the one used in *Business Venture 1*. It is hoped that few students at this level will be assessed at Grade 1 and that students will have made some progress since *Business Venture 1*. To take account of variation within grades and improvement since *Business Venture 1*, you could award a 'plus' mark in each grade, i.e. 1+, 2+, 3+, 4+.

Show students the evaluation scale before the test so that they can see how they will be assessed. Complete an evaluation scale for each student. After the test, give your students their evaluation sheet so that they see what their strengths and weaknesses are. You can also use this information to help you plan remedial teaching after the tests or to prepare for the next course.

1   INTERVIEWS

In this test you conduct a one-on-one interview in which you ask the student a number of questions from the lists supplied on page 73.

Be careful not to make the interview seem like an interrogation – try to make it as much like a normal conversation as possible by making smooth transitions from one question to another, and by asking one or two follow-up questions. Encourage students to say as much as possible.

You can ask any number of questions and in any order, but try to ask at least three or four questions, plus some follow-up questions.

With higher-level students you could have them ask you questions and follow-up questions on the same topics. Write prompts on the board to help them, e.g. hobbies / your hometown / travel / future, etc. In this way the interview becomes a slightly more natural two-way conversation.

2   ROLE PLAYS

In this test, two students (or one student and the teacher) perform a role play. If possible, match students of similar ability; if you have an exceptionally strong or an exceptionally weak student, take one role yourself.

Photocopy and cut out the role play cards on pages 74 and 75. Give each pair a set of cards. Give them a few minutes to read the cards and think about what they are going to say. Make sure that they understand what to do before they start. Students should not look at each other's cards. When they are ready, ask Student A to start. During the role play, be prepared to prompt, but only if absolutely necessary. Do at least two role plays, so that each student has a chance to be Student A.

Remind students to include the appropriate body language and gestures in their role play, and, if necessary, to stand up to do the role play.

If you give the students the role play cards before the test, do not tell them who their partner will be until the day of the test.

3   PRESENTATIONS

In this test students speak for one minute on one of the topics on page 76, and then answer some follow-up questions on what they have said. You could test students individually, and ask the follow-up questions yourself; or you could test students in pairs or small groups, and have the other students ask follow-up questions. Be ready to ask some follow-up questions yourself, if students run out of ideas.

Photocopy and cut out the list of topics. Give the student a topic card and allow him / her a few minutes to prepare. Students should not write anything down. If you are testing pairs or groups, it may be better to give out one card at a time so that students do not think about their own topic when they should be listening to the student who is speaking. Tell them that they have one minute to speak. Higher-level students could speak for longer.

Lower-level students could be asked to produce a minimum of six sentences on the topic.

TESTING TIPS

- Prepare for the test in class. Explain what the test will consist of, demonstrate the technique, and practice it.

- To assess your students' true communicative ability, do not show them the test material before the test. However, if you feel this would be too demanding for your students, give them a list of the topics and functions in the test beforehand so that they can prepare. Tell them that you will use some of these topics and functions; this should help avoid mechanical, memorized answers. Follow-up questions which students cannot prepare will help you gain an idea of their communicative ability.

- Set a time limit for the test, and ensure that each student receives the same amount of time.

- Before you start the test, greet the student and ask a couple of simple questions which are not part of the test to allow him / her to relax.

- During the test, prompt the student, if necessary, but do not speak too much yourself. Listen carefully, and try not to fill pauses too quickly or interrupt.

- If a student clearly has problems with a test item, choose another, and allow him / her to have a fresh start.

Listening test 1 Units 1-6

○53

1 Listen to the conversation and check (✔) the correct answers. (5 points)

a Tech-logics produces   cars / computer software.
b Tech-logics' main market is in   Germany / Spain.
c SB Solutions has around   25 / 150 employees.
d SB Solutions has an office in   Hamburg / London.
e Andrew and Joe arrange to   stay at the same hotel / meet for a drink.

2 Read these telephone messages. There is one mistake in each message. Listen to the original telephone calls and correct the mistakes. (6 points)

a Please fax the order form to Mary Stevens at 667-9533.
b Dan Potter called. His train arrives at 10:30, not 11:30.
c Sheryl Hogan from Jayco called. She will deliver the order on February 3.
d Mr Hamachek from ZY Designs called. He'll call back this afternoon.
e Yuko Takahashi from Bluelines called. Please call her before 12:30.
f Please send Mr Lopez the sales report on Friday. It's very important.

3 Jack Eden is trying to arrange a meeting with a colleague. Listen and complete his schedule. (6 points)

Day	Appointment	Time
Monday	meet someone from the New York office	_____ 1
Tuesday	make a presentation	_____ 2
Wednesday	_____ 3	2:30
Thursday	_____ 4	9:15
Friday	_____ 5	_____ 6

4 Are these statements true or false? Listen to the sales presentation and check (✔) the True or False boxes. (8 points)

	True	False
a In 2003 sales were over $4 million.	☐	☐
b In 2004 sales were $4.5 million.	☐	☐
c In 2005 the company sold 575,000 units.	☐	☐
d In 2006 sales rose sharply.	☐	☐
e In 2007 the biggest rise in sales was in Thailand.	☐	☐
f Sales in Eastern Europe fell sharply in 2007.	☐	☐
g 89% of orders are delivered in five days.	☐	☐
h In 2008 the company introduced an Internet service.	☐	☐

Total points ___ / 25

Listening test 2 Units 7-12

○54

1 Two colleagues are discussing plans for a business trip. Listen and mark the things they have done (✓) and the things they haven't done (✗).   (5 points)

They have …

a booked the plane tickets ☐

b sent the tickets ☐

c sent the itinerary to the New York office ☐

d prepared the presentation ☐

e finished the graphs for the presentation ☐

2 The CEO of Boyce Construction is welcoming a project team from Australia. Are these statements true or false? Listen to the sales presentation and check (✓) the True or False boxes.   (7 points)

	True	False
a You have to wear a business suit in the office.	☐	☐
b You have to wear overalls in the workshop.	☐	☐
c You have to wear a hard hat in the yellow areas.	☐	☐
d You have to have a password to enter high-risk areas.	☐	☐
e You have to have a password to use the computers.	☐	☐
f You have to work from 8:00 a.m. to 6:00 p.m.	☐	☐
g You have to have lunch in the cafeteria.	☐	☐

3 Four people are making complaints. Listen and complete the chart.   (8 points)

Conversation	Complaint	Solution
1	_____	_____
2	_____	_____
3	_____	_____
4	_____	_____

4 Mollie Fraser is discussing company training with her staff. Listen and complete the table.   (5 points)

Training course	Action
database training	_____ 1
_____ 2	ask the Marketing Director
_____ 3	call MT Consultants
_____ 4	_____ 5

Total points ___ / 25

PHOTOCOPIABLE   © Oxford University Press

Written test 1 Units 1-6

1 Match the words on the left to the definitions on the right. (10 points)

1	to expand	a	to go up a lot
2	to fall slightly	b	to offer a service
3	to attend	c	to get bigger
4	to improve	d	to go to (e.g. a meeting)
5	to increase sharply	e	to make or manufacture
6	to launch	f	to go down a little
7	to produce	g	to stay the same
8	to protect	h	to introduce a new product
9	to provide	i	to make something better
10	to remain constant	j	to keep something safe from harm

2 Circle the best answers. (10 points)

1 _____ you been waiting long?
   a Are   b Have   c Can   d Do

2 Are you going to Boston _____ business?
   a from   b to   c with   d on

3 Can I _____ a message?
   a say   b have   c take   d phone

4 I'm calling _____ the meeting on Monday.
   a about   b for   c with   d to

5 Could you _____ him I'll be late?
   a ask   b tell   c say   d call

6 I have a meeting _____ 2:00.
   a on   b in   c next   d at

7 Profits _____ sharply from $10m to $2m.
   a fell   b rose   c sold   d increased

8 The new model is _____ than the old one.
   a more   b most   c cheaper   d cheapest

9 This product is designed _____ the home.
   a to   b for   c about   d with

10 We carried out a big advertising _____ last year.
   a business   b service   c campaign   d market

3 Write the questions using the words provided.   (12 points)

1 (enjoy / conference) _____ ?
   Yes, I'm enjoying it very much.

2 (speak / Mr Grant) _____ ?
   I'm sorry, Mr Grant isn't in the office today.

3 (what / do / Wednesday) _____ ?
   I'm visiting a client on Wednesday.

4 (what / made of?) _____ ?
   Steel and plastic.

5 (how much / cost) _____ ?
   It's about the price of a small car.

6 (have / special features) _____ ?
   Yes, a special feature is the self-cleaning function.

4 Correct the mistakes. There is one mistake in each sentence.   (8 points)

1 We should getting together again sometime.
2 We plan for open a new branch in Singapore.
3 Are you know when she'll be back?
4 He's flying to Milan the day from tomorrow.
5 April was our better month for export sales figures in 1998.
6 Please to fax the report to me today.
7 The company hired a new manager, and with a result, business improved.
8 We wanted improve brand recognition in European markets.

5 Fill in the blanks. Choose the correct words from the list.   (10 points)

planning	in	advertised	expand	discussed
product	so	demand	provide	increased
business	but	speak	talk	decided
win	attract	by	on	hired

We started our tourist taxi service in 2003. Profits increased steadily every year. We _____[1] to expand our service. Our objective was to _____[2] more business travelers. We wanted to offer them a really useful service, so we _____[3] taxi drivers who could _____[4] foreign languages. Then we _____[5] in business magazines, international newspapers, and _____[6] the Internet, and _____[7] rose sharply. We plan to expand our _____[8] to ten major cities _____[9] the USA _____[10] the year 2010.

Total points ___ / 50

PHOTOCOPIABLE   © Oxford University Press

Written test 2 Units 7–12

1 Match the words on the left to the definitions on the right. (8 points)

1	to appreciate	a	to advertise something in order to sell it
2	to complain	b	trouble, difficulty
3	to mention	c	to say that something is definite
4	damaged	d	to speak about something briefly
5	inconvenience	e	a plan for a trip
6	an itinerary	f	to be grateful for something
7	to promote	g	in poor condition, broken
8	to confirm	h	to say you are unhappy about something

2 Circle the best answers. (12 points)

1 What _____ to be the problem?
   a is   b seems   c can   d should

2 There's something _____ with this computer.
   a broken   b damage   c wrong   d sorry

3 We'll take care _____ it right away.
   a of   b for   c with   d by

4 We _____ the tickets to you three days ago.
   a send   b sent   c have sent   d sending

5 I haven't _____ my report yet.
   a write   b writing   c wrote   d written

6 I'm going to confirm your flight _____ week.
   a last   b every   c next   d during

7 I'm certain that business _____ improve soon.
   a will   b has   c is   d are

8 Fuel will _____ more expensive.
   a increase   b become   c being   d go

9 You _____ park here. It's a 'No Parking' zone.
   a have   b don't have   c can   d can't

10 _____ I have your attention, please?
   a Could   b Would   c Should   d Do

11 I'm sure this project will be a great _____.
   a future   b popular   c success   d luck

12 In conclusion, I'd like to _____ a toast.
   a propose   b say   c predict   d tell

3 Correct the mistakes. There is one mistake in each sentence.   (10 points)

1 I have a complain about the items you sent.
2 There isn't any towels in the bathroom.
3 Our new product will been for the teenage market.
4 Sales won't probably increase next year.
5 I certain that this car will be very popular.
6 He have to wear a uniform for his job.
7 Do you have any advices for me?
8 Do you think we should to open a new branch?
9 I'm look forward to working with you.
10 I'm pleased that we sign the contract yesterday.

4 Write the questions. (10 points)

1 _____?

   No, I haven't booked the flight yet.

2 _____?

   No, we don't have to wear a uniform. We can wear what we like in the office.

3 _____?

   Yes, it's a good idea to arrive at the airport early.

4 _____?

   We finished the design on Thursday.

5 _____?

   Yes, I'd like a tea, please.

5 Fill in the blanks. Choose the correct words from the list.   (10 points)

forward	at	someone	with	want
hope	after	everyone	to	thank
cup	excellent	really	for	stay
glass	enjoying	probably	in	been

Good evening, everyone. This is just a short speech to _____¹ you all
for looking _____² me while I've _____³ in Bangkok. I _____⁴
appreciate your help. I'd especially like to thank Ms Chochai for arranging
my appointments _____⁵ local suppliers. I'd also like to thank Mr Tong for
choosing this _____⁶ restaurant for dinner. I'm flying back to Hong Kong
tomorrow but I _____⁷ to see some of you again soon _____⁸ the sales
conference in July. Finally, I'd like to propose a toast. Does _____⁹ have a
_____¹⁰ of wine? To the future!

Total points ___ / 50

PHOTOCOPIABLE   © Oxford University Press

Speaking test

Interview questions   Units 1–6

1 Where do you work?

2 What does your company do? / Tell me about a company you know.

3 What are your hobbies / interests?

4 Tell me about your town / city.

5 Do you like to travel? Tell me about a trip you have taken.

6 What are your plans for next week?

Interview questions   Units 7–12

1 Tell me what you do in your job.

2 Tell me about the regulations in your company / school.

3 Tell me two things you've done this week and two things you haven't done.

4 Tell me about a problem you have had with a product or service.

5 I'm a new employee / student in your company / school. Can you give me some advice?

6 What changes would you like to make in your life in the future?

Speaking test Role play (Units 1–6)

A

You are on a plane. You are flying to New York on business. B is sitting next to you. Have a conversation. Find out:
- the purpose of B's visit.
- if this is his / her first visit to the USA.
- what B plans to do in New York.
- where B comes from.
- Answer B's questions. Give as much information as you can.

B

You are on a plane. You are flying to New York on vacation. A is sitting next to you. Have a conversation. Find out:
- the purpose of A's visit.
- if this is his / her first visit to the USA.
- what kind of company he / she works for.
- where A comes from.
- Answer A's questions. Give as much information as you can.

A

You telephone B at his / her office.
- Ask to speak to Mr. Cady. Give your name.
- Leave a message. You want Mr. Cady to call you back. Your number is 0201-4475.
- Thank B. Say goodbye.

B

A telephones your office. When you answer, give your name and company.
- Tell A that Mr. Cady is in a meeting.
- Repeat the message and write it down. Say you will give the message to Mr. Cady.
- Say goodbye.

A

You want to arrange a meeting with B.
- Greet B.
- Say you want to meet to discuss the new contract. Suggest Monday afternoon.
- You are busy on Tuesday morning. Give an excuse. Suggest Tuesday afternoon.
- Agree to B's suggestion for a time and place for the meeting.
- Say goodbye.

B

A wants to arrange a meeting with you.
- Greet A.
- You are busy on Monday afternoon. Give an excuse. Suggest Tuesday morning.
- Tuesday afternoon is fine. Suggest a time and a place for the meeting.
- Say goodbye.

A

You are at a cocktail party. You meet B for the first time. Start a conversation. Find out:
- what company B works for.
- what his / her company does.
- what his / her hobbies are.
- what sports he / she likes.
- Answer B's questions. Give as much information as you can.
- When B ends the conversation, say goodbye.

B

You are at a cocktail party. You meet A for the first time. Have a conversation. Find out:
- what company A works for.
- where he / she comes from.
- if he / she likes to travel.
- Answer A's questions. Give as much information as you can.
- End the conversation. Say you have to make a phone call.

A

You are a customer. You telephone STK Sports to make a complaint. You ordered some golf sweaters but you received the wrong size.
- Greet B and explain the problem.
- Accept B's apology.
- Respond to B's offer.
- Accept B's apology and end the call.
- Say goodbye.

B

You work at STK Sports. You deal with customer complaints. A telephones you to make a complaint.
- Answer the telephone.
- Apologize for the mistake and ask for details of the complaint.
- Say how you are going to deal with the complaint.
- Apologize again.
- Say goodbye.

A

You and B are organizing a farewell party for a colleague. Telephone B to check progress.
- Greet B.
- Ask B if he / she has:
  - sent the invitations
  - booked the restaurant.
- Answer B's questions using this information:
  - buy a farewell gift ✗ (ask for B's suggestions)
  - write the speech ✓ (last weekend)
- Say goodbye.

B

You and A are organizing a farewell party for a colleague. A telephones you to check progress.
- Greet A.
- Answer A's questions using this information:
  - send the invitations ✓
  - make a restaurant reservation ✗ (tomorrow)
- Ask A if he / she has:
  - bought a farewell gift
  - written the speech.
- Say goodbye.

A

- You want to improve your English before you go on a trip to the USA. Ask B for advice. Listen and ask questions to get more information.
- B wants to lead a more healthy lifestyle. Give him / her as much advice as you can. Answer B's questions.

B

- A wants to improve his / her English before going on a trip to the USA. Give him / her as much advice as you can. Answer A's questions.
- You want to lead a more healthy lifestyle. Ask A for advice. Listen and ask questions to get more information.

A

You are the manager of a new supermarket. B is your assistant. You are having a meeting to discuss ways of attracting more customers.
- Start the meeting. Ask B for a suggestion.
- Disagree with B's idea. Give a reason.
- Agree with B's second idea. Make your own suggestion.
- End the meeting.

B

A is the manager of a new supermarket. You are A's assistant. You are having a meeting to discuss ways of attracting more customers.
- Suggest a TV advertising campaign.
- Suggest running ads in the local paper.
- Respond to A's suggestion.

Speaking test

Presentations (Units 1–6)

Your company and its products / services.

Your schedules and appointments for the next two weeks.

A consumer product you have at home.

A decision you made recently.

An idea for a new business in your neighborhood.

Presentations (Units 7–12)

Some places you have visited and some places you would like to visit.

A new product or service on the market.

Your plans for the future.

Some advice on how to be successful in business.

A speech to welcome some visitors to your company / school.

PHOTOCOPIABLE © Oxford University Press

Speaking test
Evaluation scale

Name _____   Date _____

	Grade 1	Grade 2	Grade 3	Grade 4
Fluency	very short utterances; often unable to respond	slow and hesitant; has difficulty finding appropriate forms and words	occasionally hesitant; sometimes achieves a natural-sounding flow of speech	usually maintains a fairly natural-sounding flow of speech
Accuracy	has great difficulty in forming basic structures and functions	errors in basic structures and functions often cause communication problems	fair command of basic structures and functions; errors may sometimes interfere with communication	good command of basic structures and functions with only occasional errors
Pronunciation	poor pronunciation makes communication very difficult	errors in pronunciation often cause misunderstandings	pronunciation fairly good; errors sometimes cause misunderstanding	pronunciation good; may make some errors but these do not usually interfere with understanding
Comprehension	understands very little	able to understand simple language; repetition or rephrasing frequently required	understands fairly well; some repetition or rephrasing required	understands well; little repetition or rephrasing required

Listening scripts

LISTENING TEST 1 ●53

1
A Are you enjoying the conference?
B Yes, I am. It's very good. My name's Andrew Brown, by the way. I'm with Tech-logics in London.
A Pleased to meet you, Andrew. I'm Joe Maguire from SB Solutions in Dublin. Is this your first time in Hamburg?
B No, I come here all the time. Tech-logics has an office in Hamburg. We produce computer software for the automobile industry, mostly in Germany, but we plan to expand into Spain in the near future. What about you?
A Well, SB Solutions is a new company. We provide a range of computing services to about 150 small and medium-size companies. We're still pretty small – around 25 employees – but we're growing fast.
B Do you have any overseas offices?
A We have an office in London, and we plan to open an office in Germany. That's another reason for my trip to Hamburg.
B Really? Uh, I'm sorry, but would you excuse me? I have to make a phone call before the next presentation starts.
A Sure. Well, it was nice talking with you. Here's my business card.
B Thank you. Here's my card. Maybe we can meet again?
A Sure. Why don't we have a drink later?
B Fine.
A I'm staying at the Hofstetter Hotel. Why don't we …

2
a A Please leave a message after the tone.
   B Hi, Martina. This is Mary Stevens. I'm afraid there's a problem with my fax machine. Could you fax the order form again to a different number? It's 667-9523. Thanks.

b A Good afternoon. Could I speak to Paulo Mendes, please?
   B One moment, please. I'm afraid he's on another line. Can I take a message?
   A Yes, please. My name is Dan Potter. Could you tell him that my plane arrives at 10:30, not 11:30.
   B Sure, Mr. Potter. I'll give him the message.

c This is Sheryl Hogan from Jayco. There's a delay at the factory, so I'm afraid we can't deliver the items you ordered until February 13. I hope this won't cause you any problems.

d A Our offices are closed from six p.m. until eight a.m. Please leave your message after the tone.
   B Hello. This is George Hamachek, from ZY Designs. I need to talk to you about the meeting on Wednesday. I'll call back tomorrow afternoon.

e A Good morning. Could I speak to Ms. Dean, please?
   B I'm sorry, but she's in a meeting. Can I take a message?
   A Yes, please. My name is Yuko Takahashi, from Bluelines. Could you ask her to call me before 2:30 this afternoon, please? She has my number.
   B Certainly, Ms. Takahashi. I'll give her the message.

f A Hello. Could I speak to David Baker, please?
   B I'm sorry, he's not in the office today. Can I take a message?
   A Yes, please. This is José Lopez from the Manila office. Could you ask him to send me the sales report before Friday? It's very important. I need it for a presentation on Friday morning.
   B I'll give him the message, Mr. Lopez.
   A Thank you. Goodbye.
   B Goodbye.

3
A Christine, could we meet sometime next week?
B Sure, Jack. Let's see … I'm free on Monday afternoon.
A That's not possible for me, I'm afraid. I'm meeting someone from the New York office at two o'clock.
B How about Tuesday morning?
A I'm afraid I'm busy then. I'm making a presentation to the Sales Director at 9:30.
B Well, I'm busy on Wednesday morning but I'm free from three o'clock.
A I'm free in the morning, but I'm visiting a client at 2:30, and I can't change that.
B Are you doing anything on Thursday?
A Let me see. I'm meeting the design team at 9:15 and that could take all day. I'm free on Friday, though.
B Friday? Let me check … Yes, Friday is fine for me.
A Could we make an early start? We have a lot to discuss. How about 8:30?
B 8:30 is fine. What are we going to talk about?
A We need to discuss the new contract.
B OK. I'll bring the files with me.
A Great. See you on Friday.

4
I'd like to give you some information about our sales performance for the years 2003 to 2007. If you look at these graphs, you will see that sales in 2003 were just over four million dollars. In 2004 sales rose slightly to 4.5 million dollars. In 2005 we had a good year. Our sales rose to 5.3 million dollars. That means we sold 545,000 units. But in 2006 sales fell sharply. If you remember, in 2006 we introduced a new computer system, which caused a few problems. Business improved again in 2007. We increased sales in every market, especially in Asia. Sales increased in Taiwan, Japan, and Malaysia, but the biggest increase was in Thailand. 2007 was a good year for our markets in Eastern Europe, where sales rose from 10% to 38% by the end of the year. Our delivery time has also improved. Eighty-five percent of our orders are now delivered in five days. Sales figures for 2008 should be available shortly but the signs are that it was a good year. As you know, we introduced a new Internet service for clients in 2008, and it's been a great success. Well, that's all. If there are any questions …

1
A I'd just like to check the plans for our trip to New York. Have you booked the flights yet?

B Yes, I have. I booked them last week. I sent the tickets to you two days ago.

A Oh, really? I haven't received them yet. Have you sent our itinerary to the New York office?

B No, not yet. I'm going to fax it this afternoon. Have you prepared your presentation yet?

A Yes, I have, but I'm not very happy with it. Perhaps we could look at it together before we go?

B Yes, sure. I haven't finished the graphs for the presentation yet, but I'm going to do it this afternoon.

A Thanks. I'm sure they'll be great! Let's meet on Wednesday, and …

2
On behalf of everyone at Boyce Construction, I am very pleased to welcome you here today. Before you have a tour of the factory, I would like to take this opportunity to tell you about some of the company regulations. First of all, as you can see, the dress code is quite casual here. So you can wear what you like around the office, but in the workshop you have to wear overalls. You also have to wear a hard hat at all times in the yellow areas of the workshop – these are high-risk areas. You don't need a password to enter these areas but you have to show your ID. However, you have to have a password to use the computer terminals. You will get your passwords after the factory tour. Everyone has to work an eight-hour day between the hours of 8:00 a.m. and 6:30 p.m. You should tell the administrator in your department your exact starting and finishing times. And finally, for security reasons, you have to carry your ID card at all times. Well, that's all I have to say. Oh, just one last word of advice. I can really recommend our cafeteria – the food is great!

3
1 A Good morning. Central Ticket Agency. How may I help you?

B Hello. My name is Nicole Richards. You sent me some tickets for the Tonya Hope concert, but there's a problem. The date is wrong. I booked tickets for March 19, not March 18.

A I'm very sorry, ma'am. I'll send you the correct tickets immediately.

2 A Here's your bill, sir. I hope you enjoyed your stay with us.

B Thank you. Oh, just a minute. I think the room rate is wrong. My company usually has a 10% discount.

A I'm very sorry about that, sir. I'll prepare a new bill for you right away.

3 A Good afternoon, Customer Service.

B Hello. Could I speak to Mr. Parker, please? This is Anne Harvey.

C Ms. Harvey, Stan Parker here. What can I do for you?

B Well, we ordered a new photocopier and you said we would get it last Monday, but it hasn't arrived yet.

C I'm very sorry about that. I'll make sure it's delivered tomorrow. Is that OK?

B Yes, thank you.

4 A Good afternoon, ma'am. What seems to be the problem?

B I bought this camera here six months ago, and now it isn't working.

A May I take a look? Well yes, there's definitely something wrong with it.

B Can you fix it?

A We have to send it back to the manufacturer for repair. It takes about three weeks.

B Oh dear. I'm going on vacation on Saturday.

A I'm sorry, ma'am, that's the best we can do …

4
A OK, everyone. Shall we start? We are meeting today to discuss company training courses for next year. Does anyone have any suggestions? Jeff?

B Well, I think we need some database training. We could use our databases more effectively if we had training.

A Yes, that sounds like a good idea. How do you think we should do it?

B I know a company which provides database training courses for companies like ours. I think a two-day course would be about right.

A That sounds ideal. Can you book a two-day course, Jeff?

B Sure.

C The Marketing Department would really benefit from some training.

A What kind of training do you have in mind, Robert?

C A market research course would be best, I think. We really need to increase our customer base.

A Sure. But I think we need to talk to the Marketing Director first. I'll ask him what he thinks. Helen, do you have any other ideas?

D Well, I'd like to suggest a management training course. We have a lot of young managers with very little experience.

A That's an excellent idea. Do you know any courses?

D I know a good weekend course in London, organized by MT Consultants.

A Good. Why don't you call them and get some more information? Any more ideas before we finish? Frank?

E Well, you know, we're doing a lot of business with Japan these days. I think we should offer some Japanese language classes.

D Do you think that's really necessary?

E Most of the Japanese business people we deal with speak English, of course, but I think it would help if our people could speak even a little Japanese.

A I agree with Frank. I think it's a great idea. And we have enough money in the training budget next year.

E Why don't we arrange some evening classes – let's say for three months – and see how it goes? I think a lot of people will be interested.

A OK, Frank. Evening classes would be a good way to try it out. Can you take care of that? Well, I think that's everything …

Answer key

Listening test 1

1
a computer software
b Germany
c 25
d London
e meet for a drink

2
a Please fax the order form to Mary Stevens at 667-9523.
b Dan Potter called. His plane arrives at 10:30, not 11:30.
c Sheryl Hogan from Jayco called. She will deliver the order on February 13.
d Mr. Hamachek from ZY Designs called. He'll call back tomorrow afternoon.
e Yuko Takahashi from Bluelines called. Please call her before 2:30.
f Please send Mr. Lopez the sales report before Friday. It's very important.

3
1	2:00 p.m.	2	9:30 a.m.
3	visit a client	4	meet the design team
5	discuss the new contract	6	8:30 a.m.

4
a T	b T	c F
d F	e T	f F
g F	h T	

Written test 1

1
1 c	2 f	3 d
4 i	5 a	6 h
7 e	8 j	9 b
10 g		

2
1 b	2 d	3 c
4 a	5 b	6 d
7 a	8 c	9 b
10 c		

3
1 Are you enjoying the conference?
2 Could / Can / May I speak to Mr. Grant (please)?
3 What are you doing on Wednesday?
4 What's it / this made of?
5 How much does it cost?
6 Does it have any special features?

4
1 We should get together again sometime.
2 We plan to open a new branch in Singapore.
3 Do you know when she'll be back?
4 He's flying to Milan the day after tomorrow.
5 April was our best month for export sales in 1998.
6 Please fax the report to me today.
7 The company hired a new manager, and, as a result, business improved.
8 We wanted to improve brand recognition in European markets.

5
1 decided	6 on
2 attract	7 demand
3 hired	8 business
4 speak	9 in
5 advertised	10 by

Listening test 2

1
| a 3 | b 3 | c 7 |
| d 3 | e 7 | |

2
a F	b T	c T
d F	e T	f F
g F		

3
1 Complaint: The date on the tickets is wrong.
  Solution: The assistant will send the correct tickets.
2 Complaint: The room rate is wrong.
  Solution: The clerk will prepare a new bill.
3 Complaint: The photocopier hasn't arrived.
  Solution: It will be delivered tomorrow.
4 Complaint: The camera isn't working.
  Solution: The clerk will send it back to the manufacturer.

4
1 book a two-day course
2 a market research course
3 a management training course
4 Japanese language classes
5 arrange some evening classes

Written test 2

1
1 f	2 h	3 d
4 g	5 b	6 e
7 a	8 c	

2
1 b	2 c	3 a
4 b	5 d	6 c
7 a	8 b	9 d
10 a	11 c	12 a

3
1 I have a complaint about the items you sent.
2 There isn't a towel / aren't any towels in the bathroom.
3 Our new product will be for the teenage market.
4 Sales probably won't increase next year.
5 I am certain that this car will be very popular.
6 He has to wear a uniform in his job.
7 Do you have any advice for me?
8 Do you think we should open a new branch?
9 I'm looking forward to working with you.
10 I'm pleased that we signed the contract yesterday.

4
1 Have you booked the flight yet?
2 Do you have to wear a uniform in the office?
3 Is it a good idea to arrive at the airport early?
4 When did you finish the design?
5 Would you like a drink / something to drink?

5
1 thank	6 excellent
2 after	7 hope
3 been	8 at
4 really	9 everyone
5 with	10 glass